W9-BIX-997

STORIES IN HISTORY

WORLD WAR, BOOM, AND BUST

1917–1930s

Cover illustration: Todd Leonardo

Printed in the United States of America

ISBN 0-618-22202-2

2 3 4 5 6 7 — QVK — 08 07 06 05 04 03

Table of Contents

PART I: THE GREAT WAR

1917
by Judith Lloyd Yero

Most of the world is at war, and President Woodrow Wilson has just called an emergency session of Congress. Montana's representative, the first woman in Congress, votes against war.

1917
by Marianne McComb

William Lewis Johnson lives and works in Chicago. His niece Selena and her family work on a white man's farm in Georgia. Letters between them tell one family's story of the Great Migration.

About this Book

The stories are historical fiction. They are based on historical fact, but some of the characters and events may be fictional. In the Sources section, you'll learn which is which, and where the information came from.

The illustrations are all historical. If they are from a time different from the story, the caption tells you. Original documents help you understand the time period. Maps let you know where things were.

Items explained in People and Terms to Know are repeated in the Glossary. Look there if you come across a name or term you don't know.

Historians do not always know or agree on the exact dates of events in the past. The letter c before a date means "about" (from the Latin word circa).

If you would like to read more about these exciting times, you will find recommendations in Reading on Your Own.

Background

"... it seemed only a question of a few years before the older people would step aside and let the world be run by those who saw things as they were."

—F. Scott Fitzgerald

A tank—a weapon first used in World War I—lies broken beside a road in the ruined landscape of the Western Front.
▼

The Great War

The War Began in Europe

World War I was the biggest war the world had ever seen. Nearly 10 million soldiers died. New war technology—machine guns, poison gas, submarines, and tanks—was partly responsible.

Before the war, no European country held power over the others. Instead, two groups of nations—the Central Powers and the Allies—kept a kind of balance of power. (See the map on page 13.) The nations made many complicated, and sometimes secret, agreements to help defend each other. When any country threatened another, all were involved.

The Archduke Franz Ferdinand was in line to be the ruler of Austria-Hungary. In June 1914 he was visiting Bosnia, when a terrorist from Serbia shot and killed him. That bullet started it all!

Austria-Hungary (a Central Power) responded by declaring war on Serbia (one of the Allies), and the other nations of Europe began honoring their agreements. The chart on the next page shows what happened.

The little country of Belgium was neutral—it had no agreements to go to war. When the Germans began marching toward France through Belgium, that brought Great Britain into the war. Britain had promised to defend Belgium's neutrality. Soon much of Europe was at war.

How Did World War I Start?

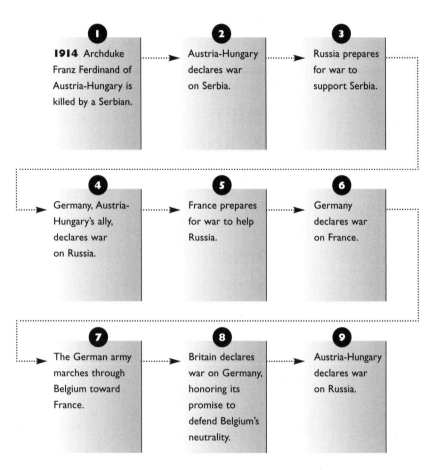

1 1914 Archduke Franz Ferdinand of Austria-Hungary is killed by a Serbian.

2 Austria-Hungary declares war on Serbia.

3 Russia prepares for war to support Serbia.

4 Germany, Austria-Hungary's ally, declares war on Russia.

5 France prepares for war to help Russia.

6 Germany declares war on France.

7 The German army marches through Belgium toward France.

8 Britain declares war on Germany, honoring its promise to defend Belgium's neutrality.

9 Austria-Hungary declares war on Russia.

Europe in 1914

Allies
Central Powers
Neutral Nations

0   150   300 Miles

0   300 Kilometers

NORWAY

SWEDEN

North Sea   DENMARK

Baltic Sea

GREAT BRITAIN

RUSSIA

NETHERLANDS
GERMANY

BELGIUM

FRANCE
SWITZERLAND   AUSTRIA-HUNGARY

ITALY   ROMANIA

SERBIA
MONTENEGRO   BULGARIA   Black Sea

ALBANIA

SPAIN   GREECE   TURKEY

PORTUGAL

Mediterranean Sea

The United States Enters the War

When war first broke out in Europe, Woodrow Wilson was president. To Americans, the problems in Europe seemed far away. Also, many Americans had come from countries that were now enemies. They didn't agree on which side to support. Wilson and others kept the United States out of the war.

Gradually, however, Americans began to feel sympathy for the Allies, and began sending them war supplies.

In 1917, German subs sank three American ships along with many other ships from Europe. "The world must be made safe for democracy," President Wilson said on April 2, 1917, when he asked Congress to declare war on Germany.

By the next summer, more than a million American soldiers were in France. There they helped the French and British troops battle the German soldiers.

In four years of terrible warfare, more than 8 million soldiers and 13 million civilians were killed in Europe. The Germans lost the will to keep fighting. So did the other Central Powers. They asked for peace. On November 11, 1918, a peace agreement was signed, and the fighting stopped.

The Home Front

During the war, changes took place in the United States.

In 1914, Henry Ford opened his factory to black workers. In 1916, floods, droughts, and farm pests caused a crop failure in the South. Then, with the war, job opportunities opened up in Northern cities. All this contributed to the Great Migration of hundreds of thousands of African Americans from the farmlands of the South to the industrial cities of the North.

One million women entered the work force, taking over jobs that had been held by men called away to war. Women became miners and ship-builders as well as nurses, teachers, and clerks. They built airplanes and drove trucks.

Disease also brought change. In the fall of 1918, a worldwide flu epidemic spread to the United States. By the time the number of flu cases decreased in 1919, more than a half million people—most of them young, healthy adults—had died.

The Roaring Twenties

In the early 1920s, the whole country was cele-brating. The war had ended. Soldiers were home. People felt like they had money, and there were all kinds of new gadgets to buy.

Everyone wanted a car. By 1925, Henry Ford's assembly line was producing 9,000 cars a day—

◀ Radio stars, such as comedians George Burns and Gracie Allen, entertained American families in their homes.

approximately one car every 24 seconds. As a result, the price of a Model T fell below $300, and the average American could own an automobile.

The radio had been used in World War I, but it wasn't until 1920 that American families could enjoy one. Americans listened to music, dramas, sports, and news. By 1930, half of all U.S. homes had radios. By 1940, 80 percent did.

Radio helped make jazz music popular. African-American musicians first played jazz in New Orleans. Later, performers in such cities as Chicago and New York helped make jazz popular. Its exciting melodies and lively rhythms were easy to dance to. Jazz was the music of celebration, and so the 1920s became known as "the Jazz Age."

Movies and radio made public figures more famous than ever before. The greatest hero of the time was Charles Lindbergh. In 1927 he was the first to fly a plane alone across the Atlantic Ocean. Paris threw Lindbergh a huge party when he landed. New York gave him a ticker-tape parade, and the president received him at the White House.

▲
In 1918, New Orleans jazz pioneer King Oliver (shown here with his Creole Jazz Band) moved to Chicago, beginning the spread of this musical form throughout America.

Freedom and Prohibition

The 1920s brought an era of new freedom to women in the United States. They had won the right to vote. They had proved they could work at jobs outside the home. Many young women took on the freedom of dress and actions of the "flapper." They wore short skirts and bright makeup. They cut their hair short and talked slang. For these reasons, some people thought flappers were shocking.

Women also played an important role in making alcohol illegal. They were deeply disturbed by the heartache that alcoholism brought to many families. They made the issue one of national importance, and worked for a constitutional amendment. In 1920, the Eighteenth Amendment to the U.S. Constitution became law. It made it illegal to manufacture, sell, move, and import alcohol within the United States.

Many people continued to drink anyway. But they couldn't drink in public places, so they met in special clubs, known as "speakeasies." These clubs were run by organized crime bosses, whose power grew during Prohibition.

Conflict in America

The nation was sharply divided over Prohibition. Eventually, the law became so unpopular that it was ended in 1933.

Another issue that divided Americans in the 1920s was the theory of evolution. This idea states that today's plants, animals, and human beings developed over millions of years from more primitive forms of life. In 1925, a Tennessee high school teacher named John Scopes was brought to trial for teaching evolution in biology class. Clarence Darrow, the most famous lawyer of the time, defended him. Aiding the prosecution was William Jennings Bryan, a three-time presidential candidate.

Race also divided the country. The Ku Klux Klan had begun in the Southern states after the Civil War. Klan members tried to prevent African Americans from voting and were often responsible for terrible acts of violence against them. After 1915, Klan members weren't only Southerners. They were also from the Midwest, New England and the West. Their targets now included Catholics, Jews, and immigrants as well as African Americans.

Harlem Renaissance

New York City's Harlem neighborhood was the largest African-American community in the 1920s. Many painters, poets, musicians, and other creative people worked and lived together there. This artistic community inspired many people to express themselves—people who were not used to having their voices heard. Their movement is called the Harlem Renaissance.

W. E. B. Du Bois, editor of *The Crisis* magazine, encouraged black racial pride. Writers such as Langston Hughes and Zora Neale Hurston explored African themes and the black experience in America. The Harlem Renaissance ended with the economic depression of the 1930s, but its energy and style continues to influence writers and artists to this day.

Zora Neale Hurston ▶

The Great Depression

In the 1920s, laws did not control the stock market as closely as they do today. Many people borrowed money to buy stocks they believed would go up in price. They thought they could pay off their loans with the profits they would make when they sold the stock. For a while, many stock prices did go up—way up! By 1928, the prices of many stocks were much higher than their real value.

In October 1929, investors became scared about the true value of their stocks and began to sell them off. More people were selling than were buying, and stock prices dropped like a bomb. Some people lost their fortunes. Some were ruined because they could not pay what they owed.

Yet the worst was still to come. The banking system was weak, and many banks did not have enough money to cover customers' deposits. People rushed to banks to take out their money, and banks all over the country closed. Many people lost their entire life's savings.

Businesses found themselves without investors and without money to get new business or pay for equipment and material they had ordered. They had to fire workers. Many businesses went bankrupt.

▲

In front of the steps of the Capitol, an unemployed man sells apples to a passerby.

The government under President Herbert Hoover did not do enough to help businesses, workers, or investors. Hoover told people that the economy would get better soon. He was wrong. The Great Depression followed. It lasted for the next ten years, and was the worst depression in American history. One out of every four workers was unemployed.

The New Deal

When he accepted the 1932 Democratic nomination for president, Franklin Delano Roosevelt said, "I pledge you, I pledge myself, to a new deal for the American people." Immediately after he became president, on March 4, 1933, he started a group of government programs known as the New Deal.

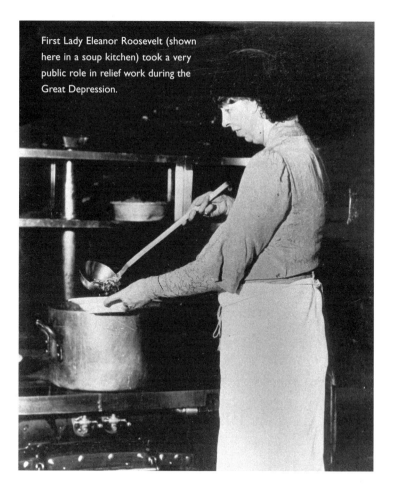

First Lady Eleanor Roosevelt (shown here in a soup kitchen) took a very public role in relief work during the Great Depression.

Some of these programs set up new rules for banks and the stock market. Other programs helped people and businesses get back on their feet. The government became a main employer and buyer in the economy. One New Deal program, the Civilian Conservation Corps, put three million young men ages 18 to 25 to work. They built roads and parks, planted trees, and helped fix damage to the land caused by problems such as floods.

Roosevelt's later programs were even bigger. The Works Progress Administration employed nearly one-third of the country's jobless. Many people saw their lives improve under the New Deal. Even so, 9.5 million people remained unemployed in 1939. The economy did not regain its 1929 level until the United States entered World War II in 1941.

The Dust Bowl

For farmers in the Great Plains, the Depression was only part of their troubles. A larger part came from a drought in the mid-1930s. It was followed by high winds, and farmland literally blew away. In 1938, farmers lost approximately 850 million tons of top-soil. Farmers could not raise crops, and they lost their farms to the banks that held their mortgages. Many farmers moved to California in hopes of finding work. But there were too many people for too few jobs. Many people were forced to live out of their cars or in tents on empty fields.

The thrilling ride the country had begun after World War I had turned out to be a roller coaster.

A Texas farm woman shows the strain of trying to survive the Dust Bowl.
▼

Time Line

1914—World War I begins in Europe.

1917—The United States enters World War I.

1918—World War I ends.

1919—Race riots occur in Chicago. The Eighteenth
Amendment is ratified; Prohibition begins.

1920—The first commercial radio station goes on
the air. The Nineteenth Amendment is ratified,
giving women the right to vote.

1925—John Scopes goes on trial for teaching evolution.

1927—Charles Lindbergh flies nonstop across the
Atlantic Ocean.

1929—The New York Stock Exchange crashes and the
Great Depression begins.

1933—President Roosevelt is sworn in and the New
Deal begins.

1941—The United States enters World War II.

chapter four

The Great War

Jeannette Rankin Votes No

BY JUDITH LLOYD YERO

pril 2, 1917.

Jeannette Rankin was nervous as she rode from her Washington hotel to her office. Rankin expected to have several months to ease into her job as a new representative to Congress from Montana. But **President Wilson** had called an emergency session of Congress. War was in the air. Rankin had to decide where she stood on the issue, and how she would express herself.

People and Terms to Know

Jeannette Rankin—(1880–1973) Montana native who, in 1916, was the first woman elected to the U.S. House of Representatives. Rankin voted "no" to the entry of the United States into World War I. In 1941 she cast the single "no" vote for declaring war against Japan.

President Wilson—Woodrow Wilson (1856–1924), 28th president of the United States (1913–1921). He was awarded the Nobel Peace Prize for his efforts to end World War I and establish the League of Nations.

Before she'd left her hotel, a reporter had asked how she felt. She'd replied, "I have so much to learn that I don't know what to say and what not to say. So I have just decided not to say anything at all, at least for the present."

She was the first female member of Congress.

Rankin thought back to what had brought her to Washington. Growing up in Montana, where men and women worked side by side on farms and ranches, it made no sense to her that women couldn't vote. In 1914 she successfully led a movement for women's **suffrage** in Montana.

Rankin impressed her fellow Montanans, and in 1916 they elected her to the U.S. House of Representatives. She was the first female member of Congress—a full two years before the **Nineteenth Amendment** gave all American women the right to vote.

People and Terms to Know

suffrage—right to vote. The movement to get U.S. women the right to vote began with the Seneca Falls Convention (1848) for women's rights, organized by Elizabeth Cady Stanton and Lucretia Mott.

Nineteenth Amendment—amendment to the United States Constitution, passed in 1919, declaring that no one could be denied the right to vote based on sex.

W hat a time to enter Congress! For many years, Europe had been ruled by a few **empires** that competed with each other for colonies and power. Within their borders, members of **ethnic groups**, such as the Serbs, demanded independence. The little nation of Serbia was independent. But many Serbs living in Austria-Hungary were unhappy. War broke out in 1914, after the future ruler of Austria-Hungary was killed by a Serbian terrorist.

Austria-Hungary quickly declared war against Serbia. Because of **alliances**, soon most of the nations of Europe lined up on either side of the war. Britain, France, and Russia battled against Germany, Austria-Hungary, and the Ottoman Empire. In the end, about 30 nations were drawn into the conflict that became known as **World War I**.

Since 1914, Americans had stayed out of the war. Many Americans saw it as a European problem. President Wilson tried to get the countries to work together toward peace. Jeannette Rankin strongly supported Wilson's position. She believed

---

People and Terms to Know

empires—groups of states or territories under one ruler.

ethnic groups—people with a language, customs, and history in common.

alliances—agreements among groups of nations or people to support one another or work together toward a common goal.

World War I—(1914–1918) war that involved more countries and caused greater destruction than any previous war. Nearly ten million troops died. The war cost the fighting nations more than $300 billion.

that war was a stupid way to solve problems. But by 1917, the call for America to enter the war was becoming louder.

President Wilson had called this special session of Congress after learning about German threats against the United States. He now believed that the country had to enter the war to protect Americans, many of whom had already been attacked on the seas. Soon he would tell the members of Congress how he felt and see how many of them shared his beliefs.

As she got out of her cab at the House Office Building, Rankin was cheered by crowds of people. Photographers pushed and shoved to get pictures of her. She hurried to her office, but even there, people swarmed to see the first woman in Congress. People on both sides of the war issue urged her to vote their way.

Jeannette Rankin could barely get away to make the trip to the Capitol. Her fellow representatives stood and cheered when she entered the room. They did the same thing when her name was called during roll call. She bowed graciously and took her seat among the rows of men.

Later that day, President Wilson spoke to a **joint session** of Congress. He did not feel good about asking Americans to join the war against Germany, but he explained that he had no choice. He said that it was time to fight for the right of nations to choose their way of life.

"The world must be made safe for democracy."

"The world must be made safe for democracy," he said. Congress applauded wildly. Wilson later said, "Think what it was they were applauding. My message today was a message of death for our young men. How strange it seems to applaud that."

Congresswoman Rankin agreed. Her feelings against war were well-known. She was tired of people who told her, "There's always been war and always will be, so you might as well vote for it."

Four days later, when the vote to enter the war was taken, she was deeply troubled. Arguments for both sides ran through her mind.

Her brother had told her that a "no" vote would end her career. She also remembered how some women claimed that a "no" vote by her would show the world that women were weak.

People and Terms to Know

joint session—meeting at which members of both the House of Representatives and the Senate are present.

Woodrow Wilson delivering his war message to Congress on April 2, 1917.

Congresswoman Rankin had seen photographs of the death and destruction that had already taken place in Europe. She also thought of the poor whose needs would be ignored while lawmakers thought only about war.

Most importantly, she recalled her deepest belief—that war was never the answer. Later in life she would sum up this belief: "If you are against war, you are against war regardless of what happens. It's a wrong method of trying to settle a dispute. I can't settle a dispute with a young man by shooting him.

The nation can't settle a dispute with another nation by killing their young men."

But when her name was called on the vote that would take America into World War I, Rankin did not respond. Before the second vote, a senior member of Congress told her, "Little woman, you cannot afford not to vote. You represent the womanhood of the country in the American Congress. I shall not advise you how to vote, but you should vote one way or the other."

During the second roll call, Rankin softly responded, "I want to stand by my country, but I cannot vote for war. I vote no."

Later when asked about Wilson's call to "save the world for democracy," she replied, "Small use will it be to save democracy for the race if we cannot at the same time save the race for democracy."

Rankin wasn't alone. Forty-nine other representatives joined her in voting against war. But immediately after the vote, her brother told her that she would never be reelected. "I'm not interested in that," she replied. "All I'm interested in is what they will say fifty years from now."

Throughout her four years as a representative, Rankin fought for the issues she believed were important. She introduced a bill for women's suffrage that was passed by the House of Representatives. She fought for better health care for mothers and children. But when she ran for a second term, people voted against her because of her vote against the war.

Miss Rankin replied, "You can no more win a war than you can win an earthquake."

QUESTIONS TO CONSIDER

1. Why was Jeannette Rankin nervous about her first day in Congress?

2. What were some of the reasons for World War I?

3. Why did Rankin vote against America's entry into the war?

4. Why do you think the people of Montana did not reelect Rankin after she voted against the war?

5. What are some other ways that Rankin might have suggested to solve disputes between nations besides war?

Moving Toward the Promised Land

BY MARIANNE McCOMB

Chicago, Illinois

May 1917

To My Sweet Niece Selena,

Well it's been near two months now since your Auntie and me moved to Chicago, and I will tell you truthfully that the North is indeed the Promised Land. Here a black man can work for wages and keep what he's earned. There's no **sharecropper** boss standing ready to grab cotton out of your bag, food out of your mouth, or wood out of your cookstove.

People and Terms to Know

sharecropper—person who farms land for the owner in return for part of the crops.

Your Auntie and me got ourselves a little apartment in a row house on the South Side of Chicago. I have a job at the **stockyard** nearby. The apartment ain't much to speak of, and if there are better jobs around, I'd be glad to hear of them. But we've made a start for ourselves, and that's what counts.

There's a reason all those black families are leaving the South and riding the rails up here.

Selena, tell that stubborn father of yours to sell the furniture piece by piece until he's got the money to bring your mother, your brother T.J., and your own sweet self North. There's a reason all those black families are leaving the South and riding the rails up here. That reason is freedom, the likes of which no Southern black people have ever dreamed of. You go ahead and tell your father what I said.

From your uncle,
William Lewis Johnson

* * *

People and Terms to Know

stockyard—place with pens and sheds to keep cattle, sheep, hogs, and horses before shipping or slaughtering them. Chicago had a great many stockyards in the early 1900s.

Macon County, Georgia
June 1917

Dear Uncle Will,

I got your letter and passed it around and around. I guess just about everyone wanted a chance to read about you and Auntie. When I read it out loud to Daddy and Mama, they listened real carefully to every word. But Daddy kind of laughed at the part about us coming to live in Chicago and said we'd be better off staying right here.

The cotton looks good and strong this year. Daddy says it'll be a big harvest if the weather holds. Yesterday the plantation boss came and looked at the cotton and said he was gonna have to raise our rent. Daddy was mad when he heard that, but didn't say a word. He knows better than to argue with a white man.

Love from
Selena

*   *   *

Chicago
June 1917

Niece Selena,

Your Daddy won't never get ahead, no matter how good the cotton crop is. That's the way it is in the South. Go ahead and read him the truth just like I wrote it.

Here in the North there's some jobs for black men and women if they have a mind to work. The best jobs are for the white people, of course. That's the same as in the South. But maybe that will change too. You see, in the North, there's a feeling that black men can save money, help each other, and one day have an equality with white people. Now, your Daddy knows that's not what most folks think in the South.

Let me give you an example of what I'm talking about. I think I told you that the stockyard job is not the greatest, but it does give me a chance to make new friends. Yesterday some of the boys there were talking about an important newspaper called _The Defender_. Someone had a copy with him, so I read

People and Terms to Know

The Defender—most influential African-American newspaper in the U.S. during the early 20th century. It played a leading role in the migration of African Americans from the South to the North.

▲
This painting by African-American artist Jacob Lawrence (1917–2000) shows migrants leaving the South to seek jobs in the industrial North.

a little here and there. These articles were all about how black men should have the same rights as white men. The newspaper says we have to fight for those rights every day of our lives. I want your Daddy to hear what this paper has to say, so I'm sending along a copy.

Your uncle,
William Lewis Johnson

*   *   *

Macon County, Georgia
July 1917

Dear Uncle Will,

I showed Daddy the newspaper you sent. He had me read it aloud so many times that I've near memorized it. He likes the ideas in it, I can tell. But he also wonders what will happen when some white people in the North realize that black folks are moving up in the world. He says that things look good for you now, but it's only a matter of time before race trouble starts up North too.

Mama and I feel a little different. We especially liked the article about **Wendell Phillips** High School in Chicago. Is it really true that blacks and whites sit in the very same classroom? I know that there are a few schools like that, but I can't picture that ever happening down here.

Your niece,
Selena

People and Terms to Know

Wendell Phillips—(1811–1884) crusader who spoke about the evils of slavery in the years leading up to the Civil War. A Chicago high school is named for him.

P. S. The cotton crop's still looking good. We pray the weather holds.

*   *   *

Chicago
August 1917

Dear Niece Selena,

Tell your father there's no point in waiting for this year's cotton crop or any other. The planter boss'll take most of the crop for hisself, just as he's done every year since your Daddy and I were boys. Your Daddy had best come to Chicago now, and leave the harvesting for someone else.

That school you asked about would be just right for you and T. J. You're right, it is one of the few in the country with white and black children learning together. We'll see if we can register you first thing when you get here.

Your loving uncle,
William Lewis Johnson

*   *   *

Macon County, Georgia
September 1917

Dear Uncle Will,

This morning, Daddy found a few **boll weevils** in the cotton. By sundown today, the plants in the field were all half-chewed. Those boll weevils are eating the cotton faster than we pick it. Mama, T.J., and I spent the day in the fields just trying to protect the cotton, but it's a loser's battle. Tonight I'll dream of those weevils crunching their way through our future.

Your niece,
Selena

*   *   *

Chicago
September 1917

Dear Selena,

I'm sorry to hear about the cotton crop. You be a good girl and help your Mama and give the

---

People and Terms to Know

boll weevils—small, grayish, long-snouted beetles that lay their eggs in cotton bolls or buds, causing great damage.

---

enclosed letter to your Daddy. Ask him to find a grown-up to read it to him.

Your uncle,
William Lewis Johnson

* * *

Chicago
September 1917

Dear Brother,

I'm writing to you directly, because what I have to say ain't for Selena's ears. I know because of the boll weevils that you may be thinking about coming up here now. But I have to tell you, Brother, that I might have stretched the truth a bit when I was writing to Selena. Chicago is a good place, don't get me wrong, but it ain't grand, and it ain't easy for a black man to get by.

Chicago is a good place, don't get me wrong, but it ain't grand.

I know what I'm about, so I'll tell it to you frankly. On Sundays, Jessie and me go over to the train station to help out. There's so many people coming North now that they're calling this the

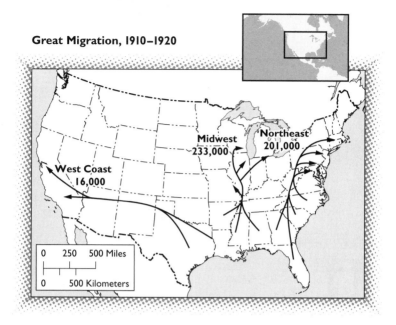

Great Migration, 1910–1920

Midwest
233,000

Northeast
201,000

West Coast
16,000

0   250   500 Miles

0   500 Kilometers

<u>**Great Migration**</u>. But I ain't seen much that's great about it. Every day, hundreds of black families arrive looking for food, a place to stay, and jobs. There's not enough to go around, and some people are living in the street.

You best wait until I can find a job for you before you come. I'll ask at the stockyard first thing. If there are no jobs open, I'll ask around. Then when you all come, you'll have a way to make some money right away. With so many men heading off to Europe to fight in this Great War, there should be

---

People and Terms to Know

Great Migration—massive movement of African Americans from the South to the North in the early part of the 20th century. Most families came in search of work and freedom.

places that are hiring. You know you can trust me to do my best by you.

Your brother,
Will

*   *   *

Macon County, Georgia
October 1917

D̲ear Uncle,

There's been some trouble on the other side of Macon County. I heard Daddy talking about a **lynching**. I don't know if any members of the **Ku Klux Klan** were involved or not. The victim was some boy no older than T.J. They say he was disrespecting a white man, but I know that can't be true. That boy is as fine as our T.J. He wouldn't do nothing wrong.

Now Mama won't let me or T.J. out of the house except to go to the fields. All day long Mama has dark circles under her eyes and her mouth is all

---

People and Terms to Know

lynching—putting an accused person to death, usually by hanging, without a lawful trial.
Ku Klux Klan—secret organization violently opposed to African Americans, Jews, Catholics, and foreigners.

scrunched up tight and angry-looking. Daddy keeps checking on T.J. to make sure he's home safe.

Selena

*   *   *

Macon County, Georgia
October 1917

Dear Uncle Will,

First thing this morning, Daddy set off for town. He sold the mule and the plow. He sold the old bed too, and the last of the dishes. Then he took all that money and bought two train tickets to Chicago for me and T.J. He says it ain't safe for us in the South anymore. Daddy and Mama will come later, just as soon as they can get the train fare together.

I'm scared to be going to Chicago without Daddy and Mama, but Daddy says you'll take care of us. Daddy and Mama are too busy to write. They're cleaning the fields and getting things ready for the move.

They said to tell you that you can expect us on the Sunday evening train from Georgia.

Love,
Selena

*　　*　　*

Chicago

October 1917

Dearest Mama and Daddy,

Me and T.J. are safe in Chicago. Uncle Will and Auntie met us at the train and gave us a bed in their house.

There's so much to tell about life in the North! Chicago is a big city. It smells funny, and most everything is covered in dirt and grime. Sometimes the sky is gray with soot all day. But Daddy and Mama, there really is freedom here. Now I understand why Uncle keeps calling the North the "Promised Land."

T.J. and me are counting the days 'til you come.

Your loving daughter,

Selena

QUESTIONS TO CONSIDER

1. What hardships do Selena and her family face in the South?

2. What reasons does Uncle William give to convince Selena and her family to move North?

3. Which character in the story—Selena or Uncle Will—do you find it easier to relate to? Why?

4. Why is this period in history called "the Great Migration"?

Sergeant York Captures a "Few" Germans

BY WALTER HAZEN

$\underline{\text{A}}$lvin York didn't want to go to war. When he got his draft notice, he wrote something on the back like "Don't want to!" and sent it back to his draft board. Alvin objected to going into the army because his religion taught him that it was wrong to kill.

Well, the draft board around Pall Mall, Tennessee, thought differently. Alvin belonged to a religious group that was not recognized as an "official" church, and the Draft Board said he had to go. So he went—but he didn't like it.

And that's how I met Alvin. We were both drafted in November 1917 and sent to Camp

---

People and Terms to Know

Alvin York—(1887–1964) American hero of World War I. As a corporal, he captured 132 Germans almost singlehandedly.

Sergeant Alvin York stands in front of the hill where he captured 132 Germans in October 1918.

Gordon, Georgia, for training. You wouldn't think that we would become friends. I was a 19-year-old college student from Albany, New York. Alvin was 30 years old and had quit school after the third grade. We had nothing in common. I was drawn to his humble country manners and plain-speaking way of expressing himself. To me, he became like a big brother.

While in basic training, Alvin amazed everyone with his shooting skills. That's because back home he was a hunter who competed in shooting contests. Still he swore he could never fire a weapon to kill another person. It took a lot of talking on our captain's part to convince him that fighting was sometimes necessary to protect the things that are important to us.

In fact, I don't think our captain did the job alone. Alvin spent a lot of time talking to his pastor. Of course I don't know what they said exactly. That was a matter of Alvin's private beliefs, and we kept it that way. Perhaps they discussed the idea of a "**just war**," so that Alvin understood how people throughout history could stay religious and still defend their

People and Terms to Know

just war—war that is morally right. Most people agree that a war fought by a nation to defend itself or others is a just war.

countries. I don't know. We would talk about everything else, like how the mountains in Tennessee were different from those in New York. We wondered what it would be like in France, since neither of us had ever been out of the country before. But we never talked about religion.

We wondered what it would be like in France, since neither of us had ever been out of the country before.

For that matter, we never talked much about the war itself. I guess we both figured there was no point talking about it all the time like some of the other guys—we would be in it soon enough. Later on we could talk about it, if we wanted to—and if we survived! We finished training and were assigned to Company G of the 328th Infantry Regiment, 82nd Division. We left for France on May 1, 1918, and arrived there on May 21. Boy, was I happy to get off that ship! I was seasick all the way.

Until July, we trained in France with British forces. We got along fine with them. Along with the French, we all had a common enemy: the Germans. We didn't see our first action until early September.

During those first few weeks, Alvin was just another **infantry** soldier. He got tired like the rest of us. He got homesick like the rest of us. And he shot at Germans like the rest of us.

I think seeing men lose their lives was what made Alvin York into an incredible soldier.

But I think during this time, Alvin was changing inside. Sure, back in the States he had already known that he would have to go against his earlier beliefs. Now he was actually doing it. Killing, I mean. We saw men we knew—friends we had made over many months—die from German bullets. I think seeing men lose their lives was what made Alvin York into an incredible soldier.

You see, I think what finally clicked for Alvin was that, much as he hated shooting at his fellow man, he was at the same time *saving* his fellow man. I'm talking about the soldiers next to him, most of whom were from the South like he was—Georgia, Alabama, places like that.

And then there was me, the guy in the company who felt he understood Alvin better than anyone else. Now, I don't know if you've ever been in a war

People and Terms to Know

infantry—referring to soldiers who fight on foot, usually with light weapons.

or not, but believe me, you can't help feeling like a brother to those serving with you. Every time Alvin fired his rifle, he was protecting me. Every time I fired mine, I was protecting him.

So on the outside, he didn't particularly stand out from the rest of us. I'm sure our company commander, Lieutenant Woods, saw Alvin as just another soldier going about his job. But on October 8, he performed such an act of bravery that it made him a hero and later won him the **Medal of Honor**. I am proud that I was with him on that day and that I lived to write about what he did.

On the morning of October 8, 1918, our company was pinned down near Châtel-Chéhéry in the **Argonne Forest**. German machine-gun fire from several places made it impossible for us to move. So Sergeant Bernard Early picked sixteen of us to sneak around behind the Germans and knock out those machine guns. Alvin and I were among the sixteen.

People and Terms to Know

Medal of Honor—medal awarded for outstanding bravery in wartime.

Argonne Forest—forest in northeast France that was the site of an important World War I battle.

Things started out well at first. After getting behind the German lines, we came upon a dozen enemy soldiers who were eating breakfast. We quickly captured them, along with a major. But then other Germans on a nearby hill saw what was happening, and they swung their guns around and let us have it. In a flash, Sergeant Early and a bunch of our guys were cut down. I looked around and counted only seven of us left.

Other Germans on a nearby hill saw what was happening, and they swung their guns around and let us have it.

That's when Alvin swung into action. Looking back now, I think that shouldn't have surprised me. All of the leadership qualities he had kept hidden quickly came to the surface. While the rest of us hugged the ground, Alvin starting picking off Germans. I know that may sound crude, but that's just what he did.

Every time a machine gunner lifted his head from behind his protective sandbag, Alvin aimed and fired. He killed about a dozen of them in a matter of minutes. Then six of them leaped from a trench—led by a major—and charged right at him with fixed bayonets.

American soldiers escort German prisoners of war.

"They had about twenty-five yards to come and they were coming right smart," Alvin later recalled. "I only had about half a clip left in my rifle, but I had my pistol ready."

Alvin explained to me, and everyone else, that he picked off the charging Germans just like he used to shoot wild turkeys back in Tennessee. He wasn't trying to be fancy. He was just doing what he knew how to do.

The plan was to shoot so that the enemies in the front of the charge would not know what was happening to those behind them. If they did, they might stop charging and do something different. So Alvin shot the sixth man, the man at the back of the charge, *first*. Then he shot the fifth, then the fourth, and so on. But he didn't shoot the major. He just kept on shooting at other machine gunners nearby.

"If you don't shoot any more, I'll make them surrender," the German major shouted to Alvin in perfect English. (He told Alvin that he had worked in Chicago before the war.)

Well, I'd never seen anything like it. The major blew his whistle and out came about 50 more Germans. Alvin ordered them into two columns, with the major in front, and we started marching toward the other machine gun nests. Alvin told the major he'd shoot him if he didn't convince the other Germans to surrender. At the same time, Alvin made the prisoners we had captured carry our wounded.

As we marched to the rear, the German major talked even more of his soldiers into surrendering. By the time we reached our lines, Alvin had single-handedly captured 132 Germans. He had also killed some 20 of them and put more than 30 machine guns out of business. French Marshal **Ferdinand Foch** later called Alvin's actions "the greatest thing accomplished by any private soldier of all the armies of Europe."

"Well, York, I hear you have captured the whole German army."

After we had delivered our prisoners safely to the rear, Alvin was ordered to report to General Lindsay, our **brigade** commander. Later on, Alvin told me what he said.

"Well, York, I hear you have captured the whole German army," the general said.

"I only have one hundred and thirty-two," York replied.

And that pretty well sums up the kind of person Alvin York was—modest to the core. Of course, that was hard for some people to accept. Some people like their war heroes to be loud and bloodthirsty.

People and Terms to Know

Ferdinand Foch (fosh)—(1851–1929) commander of all British, French, and American forces in 1918.

brigade—military force made up of two or more large groups with its own headquarters.

When I got back to Albany, everyone always wanted to hear stories that made Alvin sound like some kind of killing machine. I tried and tried to explain to folks that nothing was further from the truth. Alvin York killed only out of duty and loyalty. He didn't enjoy doing it. And of course, he was very brave, but I think that bravery came easier to him than to guys like me.

You see, Alvin fought the hardest battle of his life long before he ever laid eyes on a German. It had been a battle fought in his heart.

QUESTIONS TO CONSIDER

1. Why did Alvin York object to going into the army?
2. Who made York change his mind about having to shoot an enemy in combat?
3. Where did York's act of bravery take place?
4. In what way was York later recognized for his heroics?
5. What does the narrator mean when he says that some people want war heroes to be "loud and bloodthirsty"?

Sergeant York Gets a Hero's Welcome

Alvin York kept a diary throughout the war. In the entry for May 22, 1919, he describes being welcomed as a hero in New York City.

By the time [the reporters] had finished writing about me in their newspapers, I had whipped the whole German army single-handed. Ho ho. Those newspaper men! But they were very nice. They gave me a right smart reception on my arrival. They drove me through the streets in an open car, and the streets were crowded and we could only go slow.

It seemed as though most all of the people in the streets knew me and when they began to throw the paper and the ticker tape and the confetti out of the windows of those great big skyscrapers, I wondered what it was at first. It looked just like a blizzard. Ho ho. I didn't know it was for me until the Tennessee Society told me. . . .

It was very nice. But I sure wanted to get back to my people where I belonged, and the little old mother and the little mountain girl who were waiting. And I wanted to be in the mountains again and get out with hounds, and tree a coon or knock over a red fox. And in the midst of the crowds and the dinners and receptions I couldn't help thinking of these things. My thoughts just wouldn't stay hitched.

An American Nurse Cares for the Wounded

BY JANE LEDER

February 26, 1917

Dear Diary,

Everyone's angry. Yesterday German submarines sank the British ship *Laconia* off the coast of Ireland. It had left New York loaded with food, cotton, and war material for the British. Two American citizens are among the dead. It's just like the ___Lusitania___ all over again!

But those poor people on ships aren't the only ones suffering. The brave soldiers fighting in the war really, really need doctors and nurses. That's where my plan comes in. I've been studying on the side to

---

People and Terms to Know

Lusitania—British passenger ship sunk by German submarines in May 1915. One hundred twenty-eight Americans were killed.

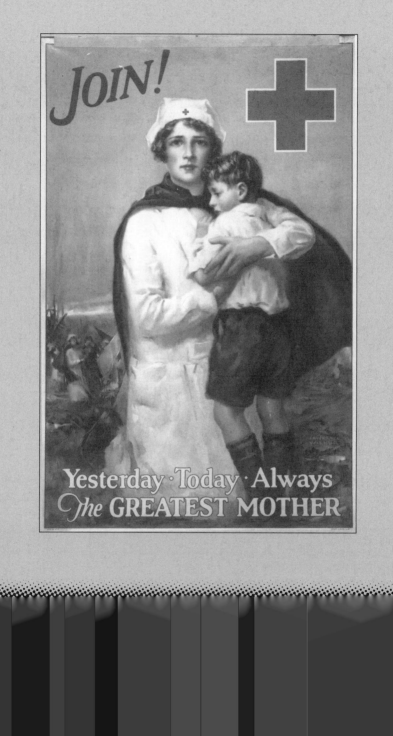

be a nurse. My parents think I'm going to get a job at the hospital up the road. Well, maybe I will—later.

Mom and Dad argue about whether America should join the war to help countries like France that have been invaded by Germany. These arguments started back in 1914, when I was more interested in what to wear to the Northridge High prom than in war.

Mom always sides with President Wilson, who has always wanted no part of a European war. They say we should help the British but not send our boys over there. Well, it looks like Wilson might change his mind now that innocent lives keep being lost.

April 16, 1917

Dear Diary,

It finally happened. The United States declared war on April 6 after German submarines sank three more ships last month. Things have been so crazy that I've barely had time to write in this diary. All of Northridge is caught up in the excitement! Bands play music in the street and people sing patriotic songs. Already a bunch of boys from my class have signed up to join the army—Dave Johnson, Bobby

Carlson, and Stu Kunkel. They're not waiting around for Congress to pass this **Selective Service Act** that's in the newspapers.

It's wonderful to think that the next time this town sees these boys, they'll be genuine heroes!

The next time this town sees these boys, they'll be genuine heroes!

Mom cried when I told her I'd be quitting my boring job at Olsen's department store and going overseas to be a nurse. Dad wasn't too happy either, but he said since he didn't have a son to wear a uniform, he'd be proud of me instead.

Now I just have to finish my training and wait to be shipped out.

April 8, 1918

Dear Diary,

Who would believe that I, Jenny Carter, am going to France! America has been in this **Great War**

People and Terms to Know

Selective Service Act—law passed by Congress in May 1917 that required all men between the ages of 21 and 30 to sign up for military service.

Great War—(1914–1918) term used to refer to World War I in the period before World War II.

for a year, and I'm only getting to do my part now. Well, better late than never!

So, here I am on a steamer going from New York to Paris. Did I mention that I studied French in school and always wanted to go to France? Of course it would be safer to go as a tourist, but not half as exciting as this!

▲
These women were photographed just before leaving to work in overseas hospitals during World War I.

May 10, 1918

Dear Diary,

I arrived in Paris. There was word that our unit was to go to a temporary emergency hospital not far from the fighting in the town of Lucy-le-Bocage. There were twelve American girls in my unit. We boarded a big truck and bounced along the bumpy roads.

The other girls and I couldn't stop laughing. I'm not sure if we were happy or scared or both. We could hear the guns firing as we neared the hospital. We stopped laughing.

Then I saw what looked like sleeping soldiers all over the ground. Suddenly, the war was real.

When we got to the hospital, there were men on stretchers everywhere. Some screamed. Others cried. Still others made no sound at all.

May 12, 1918

Dear Diary,

I was put to work right away. I had given shots to people in my training, but never to so many and so quickly. Someone stuck a big needle and a packet of something in my hand and told me to start giving every soldier a shot. The shots were to help prevent tetanus, an infection that generally enters the body through wounds.

Someone stuck a big needle and a packet of something in my hand and told me to start giving every soldier a shot.

I wanted to take my time and make sure that the shots didn't hurt too much. A more experienced nurse frowned at me like I was a child. I watched how she gave shots. She was like a machine. Nervously, I did what she did. Now I give shots without thinking about it, like brushing my teeth.

June 15, 1918

Diary—

I learned from the soldiers that one of the toughest battles of the war is being fought nearby in **Belleau Wood**. American marines were fighting

---

People and Terms to Know

Belleau (beh•LOH) **Wood**—forest near the Marne River that was well defended by German forces in World War I. The French commander ordered American soldiers to retake it, which they did—at great cost.

the Germans. As the marines reached an open field, the German machine gunners opened fire and cut them down.

Now I know why this war is so different from other wars I've read about. It was never possible before to kill so many people in such a short time! Countries keep making their weapons, like machine guns and submarines, better and better. But no one has invented a way to improve the human body in the same way. People still bleed when they have holes in them.

Many of the wounded marines were brought to our sad little excuse for a hospital. Looking back in this diary, I see I didn't mention how this hospital is not like the ones back home! There are never enough supplies, and there's hardly any room to move around.

My job was to get the injured marines ready for surgery. I washed their wounds and wrapped them in clean sheets. Then I watched as they were carted off to surgery. You can't imagine the yelling.

June 20, 1918

Diary—

Wounded soldiers keep pouring in.

I've had to remove bandages soaked in blood and mud. Two days ago I cleansed a hip cavity where a leg once was. I have never seen such horrible sights!

But I don't understand why I'm so shocked. I knew for a long time that I was going to be close to the war. What did I think it was going to be like?

July 12, 1918

We work for hours without taking a break. Last night was the first night I had a decent rest in a week. I've seen a lot in the past two months, but nothing could have prepared me for what happened today.

I've seen a lot in the past two months, but nothing could have prepared me for what happened today.

I was making rounds when I saw a young man who looked just like Bobby Carlson from Northridge High.

I bent over him and whispered, "Bobby, is that you?"

He opened his eyes slowly and stared right through me.

I reached out and gently held his hand.

"If it's you, Bobby, squeeze my hand."

His fingers tightened ever so slightly.

It *was* Bobby. Only then did I see the hole in his stomach, the blood still oozing.

I felt sick.

Bobby's breathing got shorter. I stroked his head and sang a soft lullaby.

"You're so brave," I said. "So brave . . ."

At that moment, his fingers loosened from my hand. I felt his pulse. He was dead.

Something died in me too. Instead of the excitement I felt when I first got here, there's just an empty feeling.

August 5, 1918

I thought the enemy didn't bomb hospitals. Almost every night, German airplanes have been overhead. Somehow, I thought none of their bombs would ever land here. I was wrong.

Last night, just as I finished my rounds, I heard a thunderous roar. Then there was a bright light as if the sun had exploded. When the noise stopped, I ran outside. A section of the hospital had all but disappeared. Many of the French doctors and nurses are dead. They were some of the best-hearted people I've ever met. They treated all patients with the same respect, even if the soldiers were black. That's not always the case back home, where colored people are not treated like equals so much of the time.

So I suppose now the hospital workers wounded by the bomb will become patients here themselves. I'm sure there's something funny about that. I wish I could laugh—about anything.

September 2, 1918

I haven't had time to write for weeks now. I realize that I have to write in this diary in case we're bombed again.

The fighting rages on. The more dead and wounded I see, the more senseless this war becomes. Yes, I am proud of all the men who have taken up arms to support their freedom, but there must be a better way to solve differences between countries.

I came to France with stars in my eyes. War seemed so exciting, and I was going to do my part to help. What a silly young woman I was!

November 12, 1918

I just heard that the war's over. The United States, Great Britain, France, and their allies have won. Germany has agreed to leave the countries it invaded.

My unit is dismissed, and the hospital will be closed. I'm going home. It feels like I've been away for years and years.

*I'm going home.
It feels like
I've been away for
years and years.*

December 18, 1918

Dear Diary,

My family and friends say I'm lucky to be alive. I guess I am. But I can't stop thinking about the millions of soldiers who didn't make it home. Dave Johnson and Stu Kunkel returned a couple of days ago, but no one has seen Stu. Someone told me that he's suffering from **shell shock**.

People and Terms to Know

shell shock—condition suffered by many World War I soldiers who were not able to return to normal life. Shells were the kind of ammunition used by the large guns. Being close to their constant explosions was thought to have damaged the soldiers' minds.

Mr. Olsen gave me back my old job at the department store. I'm sure I'll return to nursing some day, but for now it's nice to take a break. Today Mrs. Carlson came to my cash register to pay for some Christmas presents. She looked a lot older than I remembered her from graduation.

She said, "Aren't you Jenny Carter?"

I said, "Yes, ma'am. I hope you have a good holiday," but I didn't look her in the eye.

I guess I'm ashamed that I never wrote to her or Mr. Carlson. I never told them about how brave Bobby was, and how he didn't suffer long. They have a right to know.

Yes, I'll write them a letter in a week or two. Now isn't the time. I don't want them to go to the mailbox and think that my letter is a Christmas card.

QUESTIONS TO CONSIDER

1. What changed President Wilson's mind about declaring war on Germany?

2. Why do you think that some of the young men in Jenny's town volunteered to join the army?

3. What was life like for nurses in France during World War I?

4. How did Jenny change as a result of her experiences?

Surviving the Flu Epidemic

BY MARY KATHLEEN FLYNN

September 1918

D r. Stern walked across the army base to the hospital. As he passed by the school on the base, he saw some kids singing a funny song. The song was about throwing a lemon pie in the eye of the **Kaiser**. The song made the children laugh. In fact, one little boy laughed so hard, he started coughing and couldn't stop.

Dr. Stern couldn't blame the kids for laughing. The war was little more than a game to them even though their fathers were in Europe fighting the

---

People and Terms to Know

Kaiser—ruler of Germany. Wilhelm II (1859–1941) was emperor of Germany from 1888 to 1918.

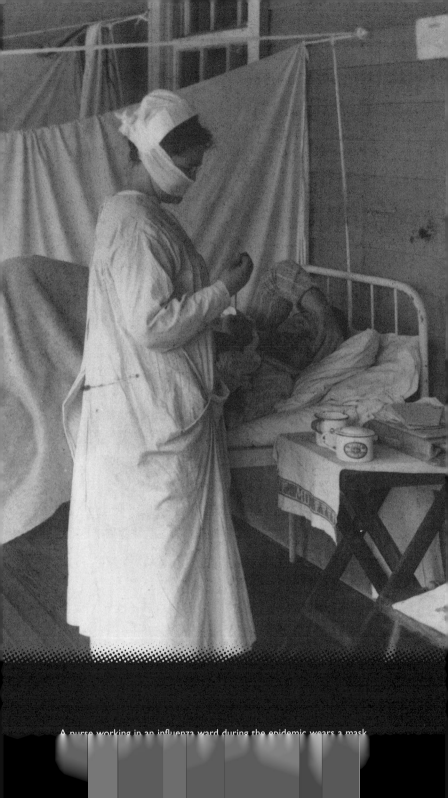

A nurse working in an influenza ward during the epidemic wears a mask

Germans. Here at Camp Devens outside Boston, Europe seemed far away.

Children were not the only ones who felt safe. The United States had entered the war in 1917 to help France and Great Britain. Now, thanks in part to that help, it seemed that Germany might be defeated. If that happened soon, America would not lose nearly as many young people to the war as other countries. And unlike the European countries, America would be spared the horror of armies fighting on its own soil.

"Suddenly we've got a lot of sick soldiers. They're all complaining of fevers, sore throats, and headaches."

When he got to the hospital, Dr. Stern checked the patient list first. As he sipped his morning coffee, he noticed that the list was very long. There must be some mistake—maybe yesterday's list was there too. Or maybe there had been some big accident that had injured dozens of soldiers.

"No, Doctor," the head nurse said. "The list is correct. Suddenly we've got a lot of sick soldiers. They're all complaining of fevers, sore throats, and headaches."

"Perhaps it's **influenza**," said Dr. Stern. "Three soldiers came in with it yesterday. It must be going around the base."

"It's spreading very quickly, Doctor," the nurse said nervously. Dr. Stern knew she was having a tough morning finding beds for all these soldiers.

The doctor began his rounds. He started with the patients he had seen the day before. None were more than 18, and they were in good shape from their army training. He expected to see them much improved, but all three were far worse. Their faces looked blue, and one of them coughed up blood.

Dr. Stern started to treat the new patients. A steady stream of soldiers kept appearing at the nurse's station. They all had the same symptoms: fever, sore throat, aches and pains, some coughs. Many of them looked blue. The head nurse didn't know where to put them all.

At noon, Dr. Stern checked on the soldiers who had come in the day before. Now all three had **pneumonia**. Dr. Stern began to feel afraid. He had never seen people react to flu this badly, and he had

---

People and Terms to Know

influenza—serious illness marked by fever, aches and pains, and coughing. It is spread by a virus that can be passed from person to person like a common cold.

pneumonia (noo•MOH•nyuh)—disease of the lungs that can result in death.

never seen flu—or anything else—spread this quickly. Was this a new form of the illness? If it was, where did it come from?

By the time his shift was over and the next doctor was on duty, several of Dr. Stern's patients had died. He walked back to his quarters. Even though he had eaten nothing all day, he couldn't bring himself to have dinner. He sat down on his bed and let the horror of the day sink in.

If it turned out that soldiers were spreading the influenza, soon it would strike regular people.

Now the question he most feared was not "Where did this terrible type of flu come from?" It was "How far has it already spread?"

War was being fought on every continent. If it turned out that soldiers were spreading the influenza, soon it would strike regular people—people who had thought they were safe from the war.

The next morning, Dr. Stern dragged himself out of bed. On his walk across the army base he again saw children in front of the school. But today, nobody was singing. One child was crying, and another was coughing. A third child sat on the ground staring into space.

At the hospital, the head nurse told him they had hundreds of patients now. She also said they had an important visitor: Dr. Victor Vaughan, from the office of the Army Surgeon General. Dr. Stern knew the visit was a sign that things were bad. But he couldn't help feeling relieved to know that help was here. If Dr. Vaughan had not shown up, Dr. Stern would have called him anyway in time.

Dr. Stern knew the visit was a sign that things were bad.

After Dr. Vaughan joined Dr. Stern on the morning rounds, they had a private meeting in Dr. Stern's office. Dr. Vaughan told him that what they were seeing at Camp Devens reminded him of what had happened at Camp Funston in Kansas that March. One day, an army private reported to the camp hospital with a fever, sore throat, and headache. A few minutes later, another soldier showed up with the same symptoms. By midday, the hospital had over a hundred cases. By week's end, there were over five hundred. Forty-eight soldiers had died of pneumonia in Kansas.

The deaths were not widely reported. That's why Dr. Stern had not heard about them. He told

Dr. Vaughan of his fears that soldiers might spread the disease around the country, or even the whole world. What Dr. Vaughan told him next did not make him feel any better. In the months since the Camp Funston deaths, there had been reports of American soldiers in Europe dying of influenza.

Autopsy results on the soldiers who had died the day before showed that influenza was the cause of death.

Things got worse at Camp Devens as the day went on. **Autopsy** results on the soldiers who had died the day before showed that influenza was the cause of death. Outside, rain fell steadily. Dr. Stern did not want to go back to his quarters. He stayed and worked another shift, helping the other doctors. But nothing they did seemed to work. By the end of the day, sixty-three soldiers were dead.

When he returned to his quarters late that night, Dr. Stern found himself thinking some strange thoughts. This **epidemic** was making the base run

---

People and Terms to Know

Autopsy—examination of a dead body to learn the cause of death.
epidemic—disease that spreads so rapidly that many people have it at one time.

out of things. First it had run out of hospital beds, and soon it would run out of coffins.

He sat on the edge of his bed and thought of all the men he had watched die today—most of them recently in the peak of health. For these young soldiers, the enemy wasn't in Germany. It was much closer to home. And nobody knew how to fight it.

As the weeks went by, Dr. Stern learned more about this particular influenza from Dr. Vaughan and other doctors. Nobody knew for sure what caused it. It seemed to have begun at Camp Funston. Then, when those soldiers went to Europe to fight in the war, they brought the **virus** with them. In Europe, the virus changed and grew stronger. Soldiers returning from the war brought the deadly virus back to the United States.

Eventually, the flu worked its way through Camp Devens. Fewer and fewer soldiers got sick and died. Dr. Stern, who was 50 years old, did not die. He wondered why. In fact, many older officers did not die, but the young soldiers did.

People and Terms to Know

virus—infectious disease caused by an extremely small particle coated with protein. The particles are often not active until they come in contact with living cells.

Dr. Stern was still worried about the flu spreading to people who were not soldiers. He called his family and friends and warned them. He didn't want to scare people, but he had to do something. Families who had lost sons to the illness were also telling people about what had happened.

One rumor was that German submarines had brought the flu across the Atlantic to harm America.

The news spread fast. Soon the only thing that spread faster was the influenza itself. The influenza virus didn't stay confined to military bases for long. On September 11, three civilians died of influenza in Quincy, Massachusetts. Influenza then traveled quickly down the eastern United States, killing people—especially strong, young people. In October, 11,000 people died in the city of Philadelphia.

Rumors started, and they made people more scared. One rumor was that German submarines had brought the flu across the Atlantic to harm America. That rumor ended when thousands of Germans also became sick.

People were afraid to talk to each other. They were afraid to breathe on each other, for fear of spreading the virus. They tried to protect themselves in many ways. Many wore masks. Cities banned all public gatherings. In Chicago, theater owners refused to let in people who were coughing. Soon the entire country feared the flu in a way it had never feared the war. On November 11, the war in Europe ended. To celebrate, 30,000 people paraded in the streets of San Francisco. Most wore masks.

▲
The patients attending a movie shown at a U.S. Army hospital in France had to wear masks because of the flu epidemic.

A vaccine was developed—and failed. More vaccines were made. But because doctors did not fully understand viruses, those vaccines did not work either. And so the virus kept spreading. Eventually, it killed more than 550,000 Americans. That's more Americans than were killed in all the wars of the 20th century combined. Throughout the world, the virus killed thirty million people.

Within months, the influenza disappeared as mysteriously as it began. In 1920, Dr. Stern left his post at Camp Devens and went to work for a company that developed vaccines. Instead of treating soldiers who fought America's enemies, he would fight this new enemy himself. In a way, he had become a new type of soldier.

*   *   *

Today, we understand viruses much better. It is likely that the influenza virus of 1918 ended because it ran out of people who could catch it. Influenza viruses continue to be a major health concern, and there is no known cure. Vaccines, also

People and Terms to Know

vaccine—small amount of a disease that, when given to people (usually in a shot), prepares their body to fight the full disease if it needs to.

known as flu shots, can prevent or lessen the effects of known versions of influenza. But from time to time new types of influenza cause concern throughout the world.

QUESTIONS TO CONSIDER

1. Why did people feel safe in early September 1918?
2. What are the symptoms of influenza?
3. How did the influenza epidemic of 1918 start and spread?
4. What stopped the spread of this influenza virus in 1919?
5. How can we protect ourselves from influenza viruses today?

Boom Years

Cars for the People

BY STEPHEN CURRIE

"**I**sn't it *won*derful?" Tim Hoff shouted above the noises of the factory floor. He swept his arm toward the workers near the whirring **conveyor belt** and smiled at his guest. Hoff couldn't quite recall the man's name, only that he was from a foreign country. The important thing was that the country didn't have Ford factories—or much industry at all. He felt sorry for the people who lived there.

"Wonderful," agreed his guest in his clipped English. "At which time does the factory shut down?"

People and Terms to Know

conveyor belt—moving surface that carries necessary material to workers who then do not have to move themselves.

By 1925, the Ford Motor Company was producing 9,000 cars a day. Assembly line methods brought the price of a Model T Ford down to $300, within the reach of many American families.

"We *never* shut down," said Hoff proudly. "There are three shifts. One set of workers for the daytime, one for the evening, one for the night. We here at Ford are always busy making cars for the people."

> "He stands in his place and the work comes to him."

The guest nodded. "How does the process work?" he asked.

Showing visitors around Ford's new **River Rouge plant** was Hoff's job, and explaining the famous Ford **assembly line** was his favorite part. Lots of his visitors, like this gentleman, were thinking of starting their own factories back home in wherever-it-was. Hoff loved to convince them to give it a try.

"Every man has just one job," began Hoff, his speech matching the rhythm of the conveyor belt. "He drills a hole, or he pounds a nail, or he mixes paint. He stands in his place and the work comes to *him*." He stabbed a forefinger at a scrawny old man with a thin mustache. "Watch, now . . . *there* . . . he tightened the bolt on that piece of metal, did you see? Here comes another piece . . . *there* . . . again!"

People and Terms to Know

River Rouge plant—Ford factory in Detroit, newly opened in 1927.
assembly line—arrangement in which products are put together in stages as they pass from worker to worker or machine to machine, often on a conveyor belt.

"Impressive," murmured the guest.

"Each piece travels down the line," Hoff said. "Every few feet someone else will add to it. Next it will be that tall man with the dark eyebrows, and so on, until that chunk of metal has been turned into a car. A *Ford* car," he added proudly. "That's how we make almost nine thousand of them a day."

"Nine t'ousand?" In his surprise, the visitor forgot to pronounce the "th." "Every *day*?"

"Every day," confirmed Hoff. "Used to be, the workers built cars in one place, in teams. They'd scurry around, grab parts, lose tools, get in each other's way. It took *forever*. This way, we save time, and we save money."

▲
These workers on an assembly line are making bearings for automobiles.

"And the wages?" the visitor asked.

"*Won*derful." Hoff beamed. "The *least* they can make is six dollars a day. Some workers make more. For men with few skills and little education, that's mighty high. They own houses, take trips, buy Fords. **Mr. Ford** has always believed in good pay for good work."

The visitor tapped his chin. "Your workers must be very happy," he said.

"Oh, they are, they are," said Hoff breezily, showing the visitor into the next room.

*   *   *

The old man with the thin mustache gripped the bolt with his wrench, gave it a quick turn, and released it. The belt whisked it away and immediately brought him a new piece of metal. Again he gripped, turned, and released.

You had to keep up. You could be fired for missing a bolt or two. Then what? Other companies were hiring, but few paid as well to an uneducated man like him.

Still, the old man liked things better twenty years ago, when he first started working for the company. Back then, it was an honor to wear your Ford badge inside the factory and out. Back then, you didn't just tighten a bolt, you *built a car*. Built it from the ground up. You took pride in what you did. Back then, car-making was a craft, an *art*.

These days, it was just a job. In fact, it was a very boring job. There was no thought or creativity. All he was expected to do was grip, turn, and release all day long. This job could make men feel like dumb machines. He could not remember the last time he had worn his Ford badge outside the plant.

It would be nice to talk to the tall man with the dark eyebrows next to him, but Mr. Hoff was in here a minute ago, and he might come back. The bosses didn't allow talking on the assembly line, probably because it wasted time. As Mr. Ford himself said again and again, "Time loves to be wasted. It is the easiest of all waste and the hardest to correct because it does not litter the floor."

How long was it until lunch?

He gripped, turned, and released. He had a couple of seconds to wipe away some sweat on his forehead. Then he gripped, turned, and released again.

* * *

The tall man with the dark eyebrows fastened a strip of chrome to the newly bolted metal. Yes, the job at River Rouge was high-pressure and sort of dull, but the pay sure made it worthwhile. A song ran through his head:

Not much money, oh, but honey—

Ain't we got fun?

Well, he *did* have fun, he and his wife. And they *had* money. He fastened the next strip of chrome to the next piece of metal. All right, he worked hard, but look what he had to show for it! How did that next line in the song go? Something about not having a car and not paying the rent.

No, in the song they don't have a car, but *we* do, he thought proudly. Yes sirree, a couple months back he'd bought himself a Ford built right here in this plant. For under three hundred bucks too! Who'd have thought a man like him could afford to buy a car?

All right, he worked hard, but look what he had to show for it!

And what fun it was to own that Ford! Nothing was finer than tooling around Detroit in your own

People and Terms to Know

Ain't we got fun?—popular song of the 1920s.

buggy on a Sunday afternoon. It was so exciting to drive with the sun shining and the wind whistling through your hair. The engine would be racing, and the tires screeching! You felt like a king, and the missus beside you was your queen.

It was hard to believe, but sometimes his wife complained about his job. She even said she might write a letter to Mr. Ford himself. He told her not to—that he was afraid of what might happen to him. Besides, she never complained about the pay, did she?

He thought about what she would write in that letter to Ford: "All day long my husband connects one piece of metal to another piece of metal. The metal comes down the conveyor belt so fast that sometimes he can barely keep up. My husband is just 23, but he is so tired he can't get up in the morning. The work is very bad for his health, so please make the assembly line go a little slower."

Oh, no, thought the tall man. *I'm falling behind in my work. That's what happens when I start thinking about my wife and her complaints. But she never complains when we get into that new car and go for a drive, does she?*

Another piece of metal appeared in front of him. He reached for the chrome. He was not behind in his work anymore. The trick was not to daydream.

It was hard not to daydream about the new car, though. And in a few years, when it wasn't so new anymore, he could get another one as long as he kept working here. What had they done on Sunday afternoons before he and his wife had a car?

That was funny—he couldn't remember.

*   *   *

"Well," said Tim Hoff heartily, "you've seen the factory now. Isn't it something?" Without waiting for a reply, he kept talking. "We make good, cheap cars, but we pay high wages. Every worker has a simple task. Sure, he has to work fast. That's how we can keep a brand new car rolling off the end of the assembly line every ten seconds! Building a car takes only an hour and a half from start to finish!"

He rested a hand on the visitor's shoulder. "So, what do you think? Will you build a factory like this in your own country?"

QUESTIONS TO CONSIDER

1. How did the assembly line system change the way the Ford company made cars?

2. What were some of the good things about the Ford assembly line system?

3. What were some of the problems with the Ford assembly line system?

4. What do you think Henry Ford meant when he said that time "does not litter the floor"?

5. What would you decide to do if you were the foreign visitor? Why?

Bernice Talks to Mother

BY DEE MASTERS

"Bernice Bobs Her Hair" by **<u>F. Scott Fitzgerald</u>** *is one of the most famous short stories about the 1920s. In it, a teenager named Bernice visits her cousin Marjorie, who teaches Bernice how to be popular. But Bernice becomes too popular for Marjorie. She tricks Bernice into bobbing her hair (cutting it very short), which was considered by most adults to be a sign of wildness. This story starts after the changed Bernice returns home.*

Bernice had changed, and Mother was not happy. It was not just a little change. No, Bernice was a stranger now. The sweet young woman of two months ago had gone to visit her cousin Marjorie and hadn't come back. In her place was

---

People and Terms to Know

F. Scott Fitzgerald—(1896–1940) considered one of the top American writers of his time. His works, including *The Great Gatsby*, have forever captured the 1920s for readers.

One of the "wild" young flappers of the 1920s steps out of her automobile.

someone who looked something like Bernice, had Bernice's voice (mostly), and answered to the name of Bernice. But Mother couldn't help feeling that her daughter was gone.

Mother had felt sadness at first, but now that sadness was turning into anger. Father, of course, had exploded right away, and then blamed Mother. That had taken place a week ago. Since then he had put in long hours at his job in order to avoid both wife and daughter.

Suddenly their quiet neighborhood was noisy. Mother looked out the bedroom window and saw a **Studebaker** roaring down the street at almost thirty miles per hour. Then its brakes screeched and it stopped—in front of her home!

The car's door opened, and laughter, loud talk, and the new Bernice spilled out. With a few unnecessary honks of its horn, the Studebaker sped off. Mother had had enough. What would the neighbors think of this racket? And had they seen Bernice yet? Would they even recognize her if they did? Or would they think that the family had started to rent rooms to wild women?

People and Terms to Know

Studebaker—popular sports car for young people. It was often raced.

Mother's thoughts went from the neighbors to her friends and relatives. It was only a matter of time until they met the new Bernice too. What would they think? Well, for one thing, they would think that Mother had done a terrible job of rearing her.

Mother's heart filled with anger and shame as she came downstairs. At the same moment the front door opened and the new Bernice walked in. She was still pretty, but the pale powder on her face made her look (Mother thought) almost dead. Her lips were poisonously red, and her eyes were ringed in dark blue. And she had cut her hair. That was the most shocking change.

Mother's heart filled with anger and shame as she came downstairs. At the same moment the front door opened and the new Bernice walked in.

"Young lady," Mother said firmly. "I'd like to have a word with you."

"You may have as many as you wish, Mother," Bernice said. Mother could tell that Bernice felt at ease about all these changes. That was the kind of thing that bothered Mother. Bernice must have known she would be giving her parents the shock of their lives, but she acted as if nothing had happened.

"I wish to be honest with you, child," Mother continued.

"I'm awfully glad," Bernice said happily.

"Are you, dear?" Then, after a pause, she said, "Your father and I are very puzzled by this change in you."

Bernice frowned. "I know. Father won't even look at me."

"I'm afraid you don't understand, Bernice. You see, it's *hard* to look at you. When we look at you, it's like getting slapped in the face."

Bernice's eyes flashed. She was slowly getting angry herself. "You really think I'm out to hurt you, Mother? You honestly think that?"

Mother did not want to start a shouting match with her daughter. She led Bernice into the dining room, where they sat at opposite ends of the table. Mother was hoping that this room, in which they had celebrated so many holidays and birthdays, would bring them together again. When she spoke again, her voice was softer.

"Put yourself in our place. When you surprise us like this, with no warning and no explanation, it feels like you're trying to hurt us."

"I'm sorry about that, Mother," Bernice said. Her voice was softer now too. "But I don't think there's any way to avoid making you uncomfortable. The world is changing fast, and I'm part of the world. You know, I'd bet anything that when I see how *my* children look years from now, I'll be shocked too."

"Oh, so you admit you're shocking?"

"New things are always shocking to some people. Hasn't grandfather been shocked by women starting to vote in elections? Does that mean you won't vote, Mother?"

▲

Magazine illustrator John Held Jr. (1889–1958) made a specialty of showing the lifestyle of the flapper.

"That's different. I'm not hurting my father in a personal way if I vote. He doesn't take it as an insult."

Bernice looked down. She was unable to face Mother. "I think I understand," she said.

"Good," Mother said quickly. She moved a couple of chairs closer to her daughter.

Bernice looked up. "But *you* have to understand that I can't change who I am to please you or Father, no matter how much I love you. What I can do is explain *how* and *why* I've changed. If you can understand that, then perhaps you won't be so shocked."

"I changed because I wasn't popular," confessed Bernice.

"Yes," Mother agreed. "I suppose that's the sort of thing I want to know."

"Really?" Bernice asked sharply. "Are you sure?"

"I am," Mother answered calmly, but inside she prepared herself for more shock.

"I changed because I wasn't popular," confessed Bernice.

"But, Bernice," argued Mother, "so many young people come to your parties. And they drive around town with you!"

"Because *you* threw parties for me that are the bee's knees and *you* bought me a peach of a car.

You're the tops for doing that, but *I* wasn't really popular."

"But, Bernice," repeated Mother, "you're so pretty and sweet."

"Boys didn't like me. I was boring."

"So you cut your hair. . . . What do you call it?"

"**Bobbed**. You're a dear, but you are ninety-nine and forty-four one-hundredths percent ignorant about the enormous amount of cleverness and energy a girl needs to be a **flapper**."

Mother suddenly felt shocked all over again. "But I don't want you to be a flapper!"

Bernice drew herself up. "Do you even know what a flapper is?"

"I know that they look hard and act immoral! And they're not very feminine."

"Mother, 'feminine' just means a doormat wearing too many clothes!"

"And that's another thing." Mother glared. "What are you wearing?"

People and Terms to Know

Bobbed—referring to women's hair cut very short (as short as a man's in back), with bangs and longer hair on the sides around the face.

flapper—young woman in the 1920s who broke the rules of behavior and dress.

Bernice laughed. "One dress, one **step-in**, two stockings, two shoes."

"Bernice! You aren't wearing a **corset**?"

"Corsets are as dead as a dodo. And when it gets too hot, I throw my stockings away!"

"But your dress only comes about an inch below your knees!" Mother paused as another thought crossed her mind. "Oh, my! Bernice, do you use **rouge** on your knees?"

Bernice hiked her skirt up so the tops of her stockings, which were rolled and twisted, could be seen. "Mother, you sound like you never get out of an old people's home! No one really rouges her knees. That's just newspaper talk."

"Really?" Mother was startled.

"Really! I am a flapper, I suppose. But the super-flappers would laugh at me. I don't pluck my eyebrows or smoke—I don't like it. And here's the biggest problem: I don't have a line."

"A line?"

People and Terms to Know

step-in—simple undergarment for women that is one piece from the shoulders to the legs.

corset—stiff undergarment meant to give support or shape to a woman's body. It is very uncomfortable, tight, and confining.

rouge (ROOZH)—makeup used to give a red color, usually to the cheeks and lips.

A Glossary of Slang

"bee's knees"—the best.

"dead as a dodo"—old-fashioned. A dodo is an extinct bird.

"meal ticket"—husband who would pay for everything.

"It's something snappy to say. Marjorie coached me on some real slick lines, but they're not me. They work, though. Boys can be mighty dumb about that."

"What started all of this?" Mother asked thoughtfully, taking her daughter's hands gently in her own.

"I don't know," said Bernice. "Some of the kids say they feel 'lost,' and that's kind of sad. But I cut my hair because it was the thing to do."

"For a little cheap popularity?"

"It wasn't cheap. As soon as I did it, I wished I hadn't!"

"But, Bernice," her mother cried, "no nice young man would marry a girl with bobbed hair!"

"But, Bernice," her mother cried, "no nice young man would marry a girl with bobbed hair!"

"Mother, that line doesn't scare today's girls. I suppose the war had something to do with that. Women went to work when the men marched off. No, not so many of us are looking for a lifetime meal ticket nowadays. Lots of us prefer to earn our own living and skip the home-and-baby act."

"You sound like all the girls your age are making these big changes."

Bernice nodded. "And some who are older are doing it too. As I said, the whole world is changing."

"You mean older women are bobbing their hair?"

"Mother, this is the style! Women your age bob their hair, raise their hems, roll their stockings, and listen to **jazz**!"

"Cut their hair?" Mother was stunned.

"Certainly," said Bernice. "Maybe it goes with being independent, and voting, and all that."

People and Terms to Know

jazz—type of popular American music; a forerunner of most American popular music today.

"Women my age—" Mother said, in a voice filled with wonder—"women my age bob their hair?"

"Yes! And why shouldn't they? Anyone who knows and loves them is sure to accept them no matter how they look."

Mother stared closely at Bernice's bob. "Really?"

"Really!" repeated Bernice. "Women today are shaking off the past. We're just as good as men, and intend to be treated so. If we want to *shave* our heads, we will!"

"Shave your head!" gasped Mother.

"I'm not going to shave my head."

"Thank heavens."

"Now I'm part of all the excitement that's happening: **talkies**, radio, **Babe Ruth**, **flagpole sitters**, and **dance marathons**. Mama, we're all roaring!"

Mother simply said, "I love you, Bernice."

"I know, Mama, and I love you."

People and Terms to Know

talkies—talking movies. In the late 1920s, silent movies were quickly replaced by ones with sound.

Babe Ruth—(1895–1948) baseball player who was the home run king of the 1920s. Some of his records would not be broken until the 1960s and 1970s.

flagpole sitters—people who sat on chairs at the tops of flagpoles, often for many days or weeks, to get attention and have fun.

dance marathons—contest in which the winners would be the couple who danced the longest without stopping.

Mother looked at the grandfather clock that was just outside the dining room. "I wonder if it's too late to go now."

"Go where?" Bernice asked.

Mother smiled a strange smile, and touched her hair lightly with one hand.

"Mother!" Bernice's mouth fell wide open. "You can't be serious!"

"Maybe I am, and maybe I'm not. The point is, you can still be shocked yourself, young lady."

First Bernice, and then Mother, burst out laughing.

QUESTIONS TO CONSIDER

1. What was a "flapper"?

2. What did the older generation not like about the flappers?

3. What are some examples of 1920s slang expressions? What current slang might have taken their place?

4. What are some similarities between the 1920s and today?

5. What does this story say about women in the 1920s?

6. What might have caused Mother to change her attitude at the end of the story?

The Flapper

In this passage from a 1926 magazine article, the writer describes both how the flappers dress and how they think.

In dress she is as standardized as a chain hotel. Barring size, flappers at a hundred feet are as standardized as Ford cars. As far as dress goes, they are a simplified national product. There is no distinction between the town flapper and the farm flapper—the automobile has wiped them out. There is no distinction in the cut of clothing between the rich flapper and the poor flapper—national advertising has attended to that. The rich flapper has better clothing than the poor one, but a block away they are all flappers.

The outstanding characteristic of the flapper is not her uniform but her independence and her will to be prosperous. She is no clinging vine. I was in the office of the president of a good-sized bank on the Pacific Coast when his daughter and several of her high-school friends burst in—flappers all. We got to talking and I found that these girls, not one of whom had any need to work, all intended to find jobs during the summer, and they thought that most of the girls in school would do the same. They all wanted to know how to make a living—and to have a good time doing it. That seems to be common everywhere.

Girls will no longer marry men who can merely support them—they can support themselves better than can many of the men of their own age. They have awakened to the fact that the "superior sex" stuff is all bunk. They will not meekly bow their heads to the valiant man who roars, "Where is that dress I bought you three years ago?"

A Writer Comes to Harlem

BY MARIANNE McCOMB

You don't know my grandmother, of course, because she was never famous. In fact, you wouldn't even say she was well-known. My grandmother was a poet, but she only had one book published, although she wrote for years and years. It's more likely that you've seen her picture, because she used to be friends with some really famous people like the poet **Langston Hughes**. I'm sure you've heard of him.

You can be sure that I've looked at many pictures of my grandmother. Some I found in books in the library. These show her in the 1920s, and she

---

People and Terms to Know

Langston Hughes—(1902–1967) African-American poet and writer who was one of the star figures of the Harlem Renaissance.

This portrait shows poet Langston Hughes in 1927, the height of the

looks happy and confident. They are different from the pictures we have of her at home. Those are from later in her life. She is not exactly happy, but she is not exactly sad either. I look at those dark eyes and wonder, What was Grandma Louise thinking about when the photographer lit the flash and snapped her picture? Was she thinking of her triumphs, or was she remembering her troubles? Because I know she had plenty of both.

What was Grandma Louise thinking about when the photographer lit the flash and snapped her picture?

Grandma Louise grew up in Sugarglade, Florida. She was the tenth child born to a family of twelve. The Jacksons lived in a tiny wooden house that sat on the marshy banks of the Sugarglade River. All year round, Louise and her sisters and brothers fished and hunted snakes in that river. Sometimes, when times were hard, they sold the fish from a little stand they set up alongside the road. Mostly they got along fine, but my grandmother once said that what she remembered most about her childhood was that she was really, really hungry.

When she was a girl, my grandmother was a better writer than she was a student. Even when her chores kept her from going to school, she always found time to write little poems and stories in her notebook. Mostly she wrote about people and places in Sugarglade. She'd never been anywhere else in her life—not even to Jacksonville, which was only twenty miles away. She also wrote down the **folklore** that she'd been hearing all her life from *her* mother and grandmother. A lot of the time she'd get in trouble for "wasting" her time writing. But my grandmother kept writing because she loved it.

When she was 18, my grandmother moved to New York City. The year was 1922. Lots of blacks were moving north around this time. Louise got a tiny room in a boarding house in **Harlem**. Then she went right out and got a job at a magazine called *The Crisis*. Louise worked as a secretary. Her job was to type up the stories the writers gave her and make them look right for the paper. She didn't

---

People and Terms to Know

folklore—traditional tales of a group of people, usually passed from person to person through storytelling instead of printed books.

Harlem—section of New York City in northern Manhattan.

The Crisis—official magazine of the National Association for the Advancement of Colored People (NAACP), edited by W. E. B. Du Bois. It was one of the most important publications of the Harlem Renaissance.

▲
Three Harlem flappers are shown strolling down Seventh Avenue, one of the community's main streets.

know it, but she had landed smack dab in the heart of a very important time and place—the **<u>Harlem Renaissance</u>**!

Louise was a secretary for more than two years before she worked up the nerve to show her writing to the **literary editor** of *The Crisis,* a Miss **Jessie Redmon Fauset**. Louise gave Miss Fauset a poem she had written, and Miss Fauset said that she might have a place for it in the paper. Grandma Louise later said she was sure that Jessie published this first poem only because she thought she was a good secretary and she didn't want to lose her. But I don't think this was true. I think the poem, called "Sugarglade River," is one of Grandma's best.

After "Sugarglade River," Louise wrote more and more poems. Not every poem was published, but a good many were. People started saying that her poetry sounded like music, like the old African-American **spirituals** of long ago.

Because she was making a little money from her writing, Louise was able to move out of the board-inghouse and into a building on Vesey Street. Vesey

---

People and Terms to Know

literary editor—person in charge of deciding which stories and poems a magazine publishes.

Jessie Redmon Fauset—(1882–1961) novelist and literary editor of *The Crisis* from 1919 to 1926, during the time of the Harlem Renaissance.

spirituals—religious songs from African-American sources.

was at the heart of Harlem, and Louise's building was right in the middle of everything! She used to watch the men and women parade back and forth on their way to the theater. Sometimes the streets were so crowded with fine-looking couples that you could barely get by. Once she told my mother that in those days Harlem glittered like a black diamond in starlight.

It was right after she moved onto Vesey Street that Louise met Mr. Langston Hughes. It was September of 1924. Over the past few years Mr. Hughes had several poems published by *The Crisis*. Miss Fauset asked my grandmother to take Mr. Hughes on a tour of Harlem. Mr. Hughes very much admired **blues** and jazz, so Louise took him to one nightclub after another. The two of them, Mr. Hughes and Louise, sat and listened to music all night long.

After that first night with my grandmother, Mr. Hughes began using the rhythms of blues and jazz

---

People and Terms to Know

blues—raw, emotional kind of music started by African Americans in the South and later developed in the North in cities like Chicago. Blues usually has a heavy beat and often features the guitar. It is generally thought that without blues, there would never have been rock 'n' roll.

in his poetry. By 1926, he had written enough poems to publish a book of them, which he called *The Weary Blues.*

After its publication, Mr. Hughes began meeting all kinds of important people. He introduced many of them to my grandmother. She met writers like Miss **Zora Neale Hurston**, who was also from the South, and Mr. **Claude McKay**, who came from Jamaica. The work of these two giants, and Mr. Hughes, soon spread news of the Harlem Renaissance over the whole world.

For several years, my grandmother, Mr. Hughes, and other writers and artists of the Renaissance enjoyed tremendous success. They were published in many of the best black literary magazines and newspapers. They spent most of their days writing. They spent most of their nights talking about their dreams of freedom, opportunity, and equality for all African Americans. It was a joyful time of music, laughter, and creativity. My

People and Terms to Know

Zora Neale Hurston—(1903–1960) African-American folklorist and writer who celebrated the black culture of the Southern countryside.

Claude McKay—(1890–1948) Jamaican-born poet and novelist whose *Home to Harlem* was the most popular book of fiction written by an African American at that time.

grandmother experienced a life in Harlem that she never knew existed. Her friends made her feel like she was the most talented and beautiful woman in the world.

You probably know how this story ends, almost as well as I do. The Harlem Renaissance died when the entire country hit hard times in late 1929. By 1930, it was clear that a **depression** had grabbed hold of the country, and few were able to escape it. People needed their money for food and rent, not to hear music or buy poetry magazines.

I think that her years as a maid broke my grandmother's spirit.

My grandmother went to work as a maid and had to forget about writing for a living. She married a man who worked at the same house, and together they had three children, one of whom is my mother.

I think that her years as a maid broke my grandmother's spirit. As far as I know, she never wrote again. Instead, she spent her time cooking, cleaning, and teaching her own children how to write. She showed my mother and her two brothers the poetry

---

People and Terms to Know

depression—period during which businesses suffer and many people are out of work.

and stories of the Harlem Renaissance. She told them about Mr. Hughes and Miss Hurston and their work. She kept this important period alive by talking about it to young people.

To me, that was my grandmother's greatest gift to the Harlem Renaissance.

QUESTIONS TO CONSIDER

1. What was the Harlem Renaissance?

2. What in your opinion was best about the Harlem Renaissance for the artists and writers who were part of it?

3. What event brought about the end of the Harlem Renaissance?

Mystery of the Dark Tower
by Evelyn Coleman

Bessie is twelve years old and fears that her parents have sent her to stay with her aunt in Harlem because they are getting divorced. Bessie is not content to just wait and find out—she sneaks around the city to find her father.

The Jazz Man
by Mary Hays Weik

Mary Hays Weik introduces us to Zeke, a boy who lives in Harlem. Zeke discovers the magic of jazz when the Jazz Man moves into the apartment across the courtyard from him. Beautiful illustrations fill this Newbery Honor Book.

Dave at Night
by Gail Carson Levine

Dave is forced to live in an orphanage after his father dies, and his unhappiness there causes him to go out and explore 1920s New York City. Soon he is a part of the Harlem Renaissance and a way of life that helps him cope with his loss.

The Scopes Trial

BY DANNY MILLER

Friday, July 10, 1925

Dear Aunt Loretta,

I promised I'd write and tell you about the big trial here. My science teacher, **Mr. Scopes**, is on trial! Today was the first day. Mama let me come down to watch the trial with my classmate Wanda from Central High. She's probably the best science student in my class, but I've never spent any time with her outside school until now. I tried to get some of the other students to come also, but they said they already spend enough time on science during the school year!

People and Terms to Know

Mr. Scopes—John Thomas Scopes (1900–1970), Dayton, Tennessee, high school teacher accused in 1925 of illegally teaching the theory of evolution to his students.

Defense attorney Clarence Darrow waits for a witness to answer.

We couldn't believe it when we saw the sign at the county courthouse: *The State of Tennessee* v. *John Thomas Scopes*. Aunt Loretta, you should have seen the crowds! We got to the courthouse at seven in the morning and we still had to fight for seats. It seems like every reporter in the country is here. Wanda says that this trial is going to put Dayton, Tennessee, on the map!

Judge Raulston came in at about 8:30. I can't say I like him too much. In his fancy new suit, he went around the room shaking hands like he was running for president. I hope he's fair to Mr. Scopes.

Leading the **defense** is none other than **Clarence Darrow**. It's hard to believe that such a famous lawyer is in our little town! The **prosecution** has **William Jennings Bryan** on its side. The whole room clapped when Bryan walked in. Even Clarence Darrow got up to shake his hand. No wonder Bryan

---

People and Terms to Know

defense—side in a trial that tries to prove that the accused person is not guilty.

Clarence Darrow—(1857–1938) famous American defense lawyer, public speaker, and writer who argued for the defense in the Scopes Trial.

prosecution—side in a trial that tries to show that the accused person is guilty.

William Jennings Bryan—(1860–1925) Democratic leader, secretary of state, public speaker, and lawyer. He ran unsuccessfully three times for the U.S. presidency (1896, 1900, 1908) and was thought to be a politician concerned with the problems of the common people.

is called the "Great Commoner"—everyone seems to feel that he's a friend, even his opponent.

Finally, with the room stuffed tighter than a sardine can, Judge Raulston read the charges against Mr. Scopes. Daddy said that our teacher volunteered to test the new **Butler Act** and that's why he's on trial. That may be true. But I also know that he really believes everything he teaches us. I feel he wasn't just trying to make a point, but wanted to educate us students the best way he knew how. And I think teachers should have the final say about what goes on in a classroom, not lawyers and politicians. Wanda agrees that this trial is about who has the right to decide what a "good education" really is for students.

I feel he wasn't just trying to make a point, but wanted to educate us students the best way he knew how.

Anyway, the **ACLU** promised to support any teacher in Tennessee who'd be willing to defy the

People and Terms to Know

Butler Act—law adopted in Tennessee in March 1925 that made it illegal to teach the theory of evolution in public schools.

ACLU—American Civil Liberties Union, a group that works to protect the individual rights and liberties guaranteed by the Constitution and laws of the United States. It provides lawyers free of charge to defend people accused of breaking laws it believes are unconstitutional and to help people go to court when their rights have been violated.

anti-**evolution** law. Maybe you already knew that. Daddy was upset that he couldn't take time off from work to come to the trial, so he asked me to take notes. He knows I want to be a lawyer when I get older.

Wanda and I waved to Mr. Scopes, but he couldn't see us with all those people.

Love, Charlene

*   *   *

Monday, July 13, 1925

Aunt Loretta,

This trial is turning Dayton into a circus! People are calling it the "Monkey Trial" because they say evolution teaches that we come from monkeys! You should see all the people around the courthouse. Some sell hot dogs, soda pop, and monkey souvenirs.

Others are more serious and aren't trying to make money. For instance, I've heard some **fundamentalist**

People and Terms to Know

evolution—theory that higher forms of life, including human beings, develop from simpler forms. The law against teaching this theory was passed by people who felt it goes against Bible teaching.

fundamentalist—believing that the Bible is a complete and accurate historical record and statement of prophecy; a strict observer of the basic principles of a religion.

preachers talk to the crowds, and sometimes I see their point. We have to be careful that schools don't become a place where religious ideas are attacked. That goes against the freedom of religion that's in the U.S. Constitution.

(I asked Wanda if she agrees with me, and she said she does, but then she went back to being quiet. She takes a lot of notes, too, but I don't know why. Maybe she's just in the habit of note-taking since she's such a good student.)

So guess what happened? Once the trial started today, Mr. Darrow argued that it's the Butler Act that actually goes against the Constitution! That's because in this country there aren't supposed to be laws that stop us from saying what we believe. Auntie, I know you and Mama don't agree with the writings of **Charles Darwin**, but I still don't see why it should be against the law to *talk* about evolution. Mr. Darrow said the Bible should not be "the yardstick to measure every man's intelligence."

Your niece, Charlene

* * *

People and Terms to Know

Charles Darwin—(1809–1882) British naturalist and author of *On the Origin of Species* (1859), which presented his theory of evolution.

▲
John Scopes

Wednesday, July 15, 1925

Dear Auntie,

This morning Wanda and I talked to a man from *The New York Times* who called this "the Trial of the Century"! I feel so lucky to be here to see it.

Today another of Mr. Scopes's lawyers, Mr. Malone (the only one still wearing his suit jacket in this awful heat), got up to speak. He said that the defense will show that the Bible is a religious book that should not be used in regular schooling.

Later in the day, Howard Morgan, one of the boys from our school, was called to testify. Howard told me before he went up that he didn't want to get Mr. Scopes in more trouble, but Mr. Scopes told him it was okay. He told Howard that he should just tell the truth. Poor Howard was so nervous! Mr. Darrow asked him if what Mr. Scopes taught had hurt him in any way. Howard said no. I guess that should help Mr. Scopes.

"How dare the scientists put a man in a little ring like that with lions and tigers and everything that is bad!"

Best, Charlene

*　　*　　*

Thursday, July 16, 1925

Aunt Loretta,

This afternoon, William Jennings Bryan waved around a copy of our science book, *Civil Biology*. He showed a diagram of a man grouped together with other mammals. "The Christian believes that man came from above," Bryan said, "but the evolutionist believes that he must have come from below. . . . How dare the scientists put a man in a little ring like that with lions and tigers and everything that is bad!"

Aunt Loretta, I'm not really sure Mr. Bryan fully understands Darwin's theories, but he sure got everyone's attention. He shouted that the Bible should not be questioned and that parents should not let teachers take away their children's faith in God. The whole room started clapping.

Mr. Malone shot right back, "Why does the prosecution fear, so greatly, the teaching of science? For God's sake," Malone yelled, "let the children have their minds kept open!" Now everyone cheered for the defense. It's as if this crowd can't decide which side it's rooting for!

Yours truly, Charlene

*   *   *

Monday, July 20, 1925

Dear Aunt Loretta,

What a day! First the judge ordered the trial moved outside to the courthouse lawn. He said he was worried that the huge crowd was causing the ceiling below to crack. Wanda and I are just happy to be out of that boiling room!

Once we were outside, the defense called Mr. Bryan to the stand. Can you believe it—a prosecuting lawyer called for the defense! Wanda said that that hardly ever happens in trials because one side is too afraid of what the other side will say in the witness box. Well, we were even more shocked when Bryan agreed! The other lawyers on his team were objecting left and right, but Bryan went up there anyway.

News of Darrow questioning Bryan spread faster than butter on hot corn.

Let me tell you, Aunt Loretta, news of Darrow questioning Bryan spread faster than butter on hot corn. In no time at all the crowd on the lawn tripled! I swear, I've never seen so many people in one place in my life. Mama ran over from the house and somehow found Wanda and me.

Darrow began by asking Bryan about Bible history. He asked if Bryan believed everything in the Bible and Bryan said that he did. Bryan is a fundamentalist too, I guess.

Then Darrow got into the story of creation. He asked Bryan if he *really* thought the Earth and everything on it was created in only six days. Bryan replied that the Bible didn't necessarily mean the same thing that we mean when we say "six days," you know, six twenty-four-hour periods. Bryan said the days mentioned in the Bible might have stood for six longer periods. So, the fundamentalist

Bryan didn't believe everything in the Bible word-for-word after all! The Bible said "day," but he read it to mean something different—maybe six years or six centuries!

Darrow then questioned Bryan about science. Bryan got flustered and accused Darrow of trying to insult the Bible. Darrow became angry and said, "I object to your statement. I am examining you on your fool ideas that no intelligent Christian on earth believes!" Oh, Auntie, everyone started yelling, including Mama! I half expected Darrow and Bryan to strike each other! Judge Raulston quickly ended today's part of the trial.

I must say, Dayton has never seen the likes of these two men squaring off. Mama thought that Bryan held his own. Wanda and I thought that Darrow won hands down.

Sincerely, Charlene

*   *   *

Tuesday, July 21, 1925

Aunt Loretta,

It's all over! The jury was out for only a few minutes. When they came back the foreman said, "We have found for the state, found the defendant guilty!" The judge set Mr. Scopes's fine at $100. For the first time, he let Mr. Scopes address the court.

"Your honor, I feel that I have been **convicted** of **violating an unjust statute**," he said. "I will continue in the future, as I have in the past, to oppose this law in any way I can." Wanda and I looked at each other in amazement. Was this really our mild-mannered science teacher?

But later on I got my biggest shock. It turns out that Wanda wasn't rooting for Mr. Scopes all along like I was. In fact, she was taking notes so she could speak about the trial at her church! I said, "Wanda, you are the best science student in our class. Don't tell me you'd rather have William Jennings Bryan as your teacher!"

"I think people can believe in the Bible and science."

She said, "Well, you know, Charlene, not all Christians think science is bad or not worth knowing. I think people can believe in the Bible and science."

"But you don't think the Bible should be taught in science class, do you?"

People and Terms to Know

convicted—found guilty by a court of law.
violating an unjust statute—breaking an unfair law.

"I don't think it would hurt to mention what it says. Yes, we should learn about evolution, but shouldn't we also learn about other ideas? Isn't that what the defense meant by 'let the children have their minds kept open'?"

Well, Wanda has definitely made me think about a few things. Now the only thing I'm sure of is that this question of whether evolution should be taught is going to be around for a long, long time!

All my best, Charlene

QUESTIONS TO CONSIDER

1. What law did John Scopes break that led to the Scopes Trial?

2. Why did some people call the event the "Monkey Trial"?

3. Why were some fundamentalists opposed to the teaching of evolution in the schools?

4. Why did both sides in the trial think that they were arguing for what was best for students?

5. How do Wanda's feelings on using the Bible in school differ from those of William Jennings Bryan?

Darrow Questions Bryan

The climax of the Scopes trial came when defense attorney Clarence Darrow called prosecutor William Jennings Bryan as a witness.

Darrow. Do you claim that everything in the Bible should be literally interpreted?

Bryan. I believe everything in the Bible should be accepted as it is given there; some of the Bible is given illustratively. For instance: "Ye are the salt of the earth." I would not insist that man is actually salt, or that he had flesh of salt, but it is used in the sense of salt as saving God's people.

Darrow. But when you read that Jonah swallowed the whale—or that the whale swallowed Jonah—excuse me, please, how do you literally interpret that?

Bryan. When I read that a big fish swallowed Jonah—it does not say whale.

Darrow. Does it? Are you sure?

Bryan. That is my recollection of it. A big fish, and I believe it, and I believe in a God who can make a whale and can make a man and can make both do what He pleases.

Darrow. Now, you say, the big fish swallowed Jonah. And he remained there—how long? Three days, and then he spewed him upon the land. You believe that the big fish was made to swallow Jonah?

Bryan. I am not prepared to say that; the Bible merely says it was done.

Darrow. You don't know whether it was the ordinary run of fish, or made for the purpose?

Bryan. You may guess; you evolutionists guess.

Darrow. But when we do guess, we have a sense to guess right.

Bryan. But do not do it often.

Lindbergh

BY BRIAN J. MAHONEY

New York, 1927

Jimmy found me in a **speakeasy** on Fifth Avenue. My snugglepup and I had been painting the town red all evening, and when Jimmy came in all wild-eyed it kind of ruined the mood for a while. But when you haven't seen your brother in a long time, and then he finds you at three in the morning, well, you listen to what he has to say.

"What're you doing here, Jimmy?" I asked. "Are you okay?"

He nodded his head up and down fast. Ralph, my boyfriend, gave me a strange look. It said, "He

---

People and Terms to Know

speakeasy—place, like a club or bar, for the illegal sale of alcoholic drinks. Prohibition outlawed alcoholic beverages from 1920 to 1933.

Charles Lindbergh

doesn't look okay to me." I didn't care. Jimmy was my big brother, and who cares if he doesn't talk as much or as well as he used to?

"He's up there right now," Jimmy said, pointing. "I couldn't sleep thinking about it, so I thought to come looking for you, Bonnie. I know you don't sleep at night."

Lindbergh was heading for Paris, France. He was all by himself.

"Slow down, Jimmy," I said. "*Who's* up there?"

"Lindbergh!" he practically screamed. "**Charles A. Lindbergh**! Lindy!"

"That pilot who's flying over the Atlantic?" I asked.

Jimmy broke out in a big smile. I hadn't seen him smile like that in ages. Ralph and I knew only a little bit about Lindbergh. We were up on music and clothes and the best places to dance in New York, but we weren't big on reading newspapers. Jimmy pushed us into a booth and started talking about Lindy like he was his best friend.

Jimmy described how Lindbergh was heading for Paris, France. He was all by himself, and he wasn't going to make any stops along the way. He

---

People and Terms to Know

Charles A. Lindbergh—(1902–1974) first person to fly nonstop alone across the Atlantic Ocean.

had no radio, so there was no hope for rescue if something went wrong. Six people had already died trying to cross the Atlantic in the same way.

"The papers call him the 'Flying Fool,'" Jimmy said. "But he has the guts to try and fly a little plane all the way to Paris!"

Now I thought I could see why Jimmy was so excited. The only way to Paris was on a big ship like the one my brother took home from the Great War. In fact, this was the first time Jimmy had gotten excited about *anything* since he came home from the war. I was just a little girl when he left to fight in France. I begged him not to go—not to be another dead hero. But he said, "Don't worry, Bon Bon. I have to go it alone for a while."

The day he left, I cried until I hated him. When he came back he was a hero to me, but he was also *different*.

"Listen, Jimmy," said Ralph. "You know I like you swell, but let me ask you something. How do you know Lindbergh's up there?" He pointed at the ceiling just as Jimmy had. "How would you know if he crashed an hour ago? He could be fish food by now."

"No, sir. I know he's up there and he's doing fine. I just know it."

Glossary of Slang

"**snugglepup**"—boyfriend.

"**painting the town red**"—
out on the town for a good time.

"**Dumb Dora**"—dumb woman.

"**cut the rug**"—dance.

"**jazbos**"—boyfriends.

"**cut the rug**"—dance.

"**flat tire**"—boring person.

"**sheba**"—a stylish woman.

"**jellybean**"—boyfriend.

His voice was calm, but I could see that what Ralph had said bothered him. He wouldn't know for sure that Lindy was okay until word came back from France.

Suddenly Jimmy ran out of the speakeasy and into the night. Ralph and I quickly forgot about Lindbergh and Jimmy. We danced the Charleston, the Black Bottom, and the Shimmy until the sun came up. Then I went home to sleep.

Maybe it sounds mean that I wasn't thinking about Jimmy, but let me tell you a few things. The Jimmy who walked off that ship after the war was like a stranger. He'd stare all the time like he was looking at ghosts. He never talked about what he did **"Over There."** But I had heard about soldiers like him fighting trench-to-trench and charging into machine gun fire.

Whatever he had done, it made him all sour and no fun at all. When I started going out on the town, he called me a "Dumb Dora" because I could cut the rug with the coolest of jazbos. I thought, "Well, he can just be a flat tire who cleans schools for a living and stares at the walls all the time." What's a girl to do, for crying out loud? Dress like mammy and get married? Ha, ha—the idea just slaughters me!

In fact, I thought, I bet a man like Lindy would like a lady who could look him in the eye and tell him what's what. Why, just one look at my fringed skirt, and stockings rolled way down low, and he'd say, "What a sheba!" Yup, if only a jellybean like Lindy would show up in a raccoon coat and a **Stutz Bearcat** to take me dancing all night (sighhhhhh).

People and Terms to Know

"Over There"—patriotic World War I song. "There" was Europe, where Americans were shipped to fight the Germans.

Stutz Bearcat—car popular in the 1920s.

You may have guessed that by now I was dreaming.

*   *   *

The dreaming stopped when the pounding on my door started. It was early evening. Jimmy was yelling, "Lindy made it! Lindy made it! Whoo hoo!" And then he ran into the street screaming like a maniac. All the cars were honking. People in the streets were banging on all the pots, and all the pans, and all the backs they could find.

"Lindy made it! Lindy made it! Whoo hoo!"

I threw on some clothes just in time to open the door for Jimmy, who was about to start pounding it again. In his hands was *The New York Times*, which had a huge headline: "LINDBERGH DOES IT! TO PARIS IN 33 1/2 HOURS; FLIES 1,000 MILES THROUGH SNOW AND SLEET; CHEERING FRENCH CARRY HIM OFF FIELD."

While I made myself a sunset breakfast, Jimmy kept talking about Lindbergh as if we were still back in the speakeasy.

▲

The *Spirit of St. Louis* was a plane that lacked both radio and parachute!

"Lindy was a **barnstormer** and flew the first air mail route from St. Louis to Chicago." Then the veins started to pop out of Jimmy's neck as he said, "Would you believe that thirty-one of the forty air mail pilots *crashed* and *died* delivering air mail? That's right, and Lindy survived not one, but *three* crashes!

"Someone named Orteig offered a prize of $25,000 to anyone who'd be crazy enough to fly from an American city to a European capital! Lindy decided that one man in a small plane might make it. Some St. Louis businessmen put up the money for his specially built airplane, so he called it *Spirit of St. Louis*. It has fabric walls and no windshield—only side windows and a **periscope** to look outside! Even the pilot's chair is made of wicker to save weight. Lindy was so careful about saving weight, he trimmed the sides of his maps!

"And not only that, Sis, but he couldn't sleep the night before he left, and he still stayed awake for thirty-three and one-half hours!"

People and Terms to Know

barnstormer—early stunt flyer who performed wild flying tricks.
periscope—instrument that uses mirrors to allow observation of objects that are not in a direct line of sight.

This was the most I had heard Jimmy speak in ten years! He talked so much that I finished my whole breakfast by the time I could get a word in.

"But, Jimmy, isn't Lindy just some kind of stunt man, like those guys who walk on airplane wings? I mean, he's not defending his country like you did. He's not a real hero."

I thought Jimmy might get angry at me for saying this, but he didn't. "You're right, sis, he's no war hero. But I think I like his kind of hero more. He's brave on the outside, but I bet he's sometimes scared inside. He's facing the unknown. And he could die at any time. Those are the same things a soldier deals with, but Lindy's doing it without being part of the fear and death himself. See what I mean?"

Suddenly I felt like crying. It felt so good to see Jimmy full of pep again that something in my heart just gave way. He was talking and acting like he had before the war. He was excited, but he made sense, good sense. And his eyes weren't so wild anymore.

As for Lindy, I guess he was my hero now too. But it wasn't because he'd flown across the

Atlantic. It was because he had given me my brother back.

* * *

Anyway, America went positively *NUTS* waiting for Lindbergh to come back on the warship **President Coolidge** sent to fetch him. Lindy was so handsome, so quiet and polite—he was a hero made to order. We had so many songs about him. My favorites were "Lucky Lindy" and "When Lindy Comes Home." I even danced the "Lindy Hop."

My brother led me by the hand through people packed ten deep along the parade route.

When Lindbergh's parade finally started, I thought New York City would explode. Ralph wanted to come see the parade with me, but I just wanted to be with Jimmy. My brother led me by the hand through people packed ten deep along the parade route. We found a doorway that shielded us from the

---

People and Terms to Know

President Coolidge—Calvin Coolidge (1872–1933), president of the United States from 1923 until early 1929. The country enjoyed good economic times during his presidency.

blizzard of **ticker tape** that fell, filling Lindbergh's car. As the car approached, it stopped in front of us—and HE got out. The crowd roared. My brother stood frozen as Lindy laid down a wreath of roses on a memorial for the dead.

"What's that?" I asked. There was some kind of flame burning.

"That's the Eternal Light. The flowers are for the boys who didn't come back from the war," he said.

His soft words brought back a warm spring day when a young man left home to fight the Great War, alone. And then my eyes turned to Lindbergh, who had stopped his parade to thank those who did something great—but who never got a chance to be in a parade.

As the ticker tape rained down and the crowd kept cheering, I understood something. All of my brother's great heroes were all in one place, and so I turned slowly and hugged mine.

People and Terms to Know

ticker tape—long ribbons of paper with stock market news and prices printed on them.

QUESTIONS TO CONSIDER

1. Why did Charles Lindbergh want to fly across the Atlantic Ocean?

2. Why was Lindbergh a hero to Jimmy?

3. Why were Jimmy and Bonnie moved when Lindbergh laid the flowers on the war memorial?

4. Why, in your opinion, were Americans "positively *NUTS*" about Lindbergh?

5. What is your definition of a hero?

Charles A. Lindbergh: A Human Hero
by James Giblin

James Giblin has written a book complete with stories from Lindbergh's childhood. The well-written biography talks about this American hero's faults as well as his success.

The First Solo Transatlantic Flight: The Story of Charles Lindbergh and His Airplane, the *Spirit of St. Louis*
by Richard L. Taylor

Learn how Lindbergh became a pilot and how he flew across the Atlantic Ocean in his famous airplane. This book also shows how the airplane was designed to be able to fly such a long distance.

Airplanes (Supreme Machines: The Stories Behind Technological Marvels)
by Moira Butterfield

It may have been big news for Lindbergh to cross the Atlantic in the 1920s, but now planes fly long distances like that every day.

Hard Times

"The Only Thing We Have to Fear Is Fear Itself"

BY STEPHEN FEINSTEIN

Mark Murphy walked home from work in the gathering gloom. He hardly saw the people crowding the sidewalks, nor did he hear the noise of the New York traffic. He decided to walk rather than take the subway because he was in no hurry to get home. Besides, walking saved money.

Mark made his way along Broadway to his apartment on 109th Street. He was blasted by bitter winter winds, but he felt nothing. He was still in shock. Exactly one hour ago, Mr. Wood, his boss, had called him into his office.

"Mark," said Mr. Wood, "you've worked hard these past five years at Wood's Shoes. So I'm very sorry to have to tell you this. But . . . hard as I try, I

President Roosevelt used his radio addresses to help boost public morale during the Great Depression.

can't make ends meet. I'm closing up the shop. Here is your final paycheck. Because I like you, I'm giving you an extra week's salary."

Mark remembered that fall day in 1929 when the stock market crashed.

These were words Mark had hoped he would never hear. He thanked Mr. Wood and left.

It was January 1932. The country was sinking deeper into the **Great Depression** that had started in 1929. Hundreds of businesses closed their doors each day, throwing more and more people out of work. Mark wondered if he could find another job. He was a good salesman, but the problem was that no one was hiring. That's because you can't sell what people can't afford to buy.

"What will I tell Alison?" thought Mark. "What'll I say to the kids?"

Mark remembered that fall day in 1929 when the **stock market** crashed. Some people back then

---

People and Terms to Know

Great Depression—worst economic period in American history. Lasting ten years, this depression caused as many as one out of every four workers to be without a job.

stock market—place where stocks are bought and sold. Stocks allow people to own a piece of a company.

thought the world was coming to an end. But not Mark. He didn't own any stocks. His world continued as usual. And then, in March 1930, President **Herbert Hoover** told the country that the depression would end in sixty days. Mark had believed him—he was the president!

However, Hoover had been terribly wrong about the sixty days. Over the next two years, many of Mark's friends and neighbors lost their jobs. Still, Hoover and his advisors seemed to think that this slowdown was just part of the normal ups and downs of business. Sometimes things were good, and sometimes they were bad. That's just the way it was, Hoover believed, and it wasn't the government's job to interfere too much with the economy. In time, it would take care of itself.

More and more beggars appeared on the streets of New York. Men who couldn't find work sold apples on street corners. Every day people stood for hours in line for a meal from a soup kitchen. But Mark hadn't done these things because he still had a job. Every day after work, Alison had a good dinner waiting for him. Sally

---

People and Terms to Know

Herbert Hoover—(1874–1964) 31st president of the United States. Elected in 1928, Hoover was in office when America's economy went from the prosperity of the 1920s to the depression of the 1930s.

and little Billy had nice clean clothes to wear to school. All in all, the Murphy family had been doing rather well—until now.

Waiting to cross the street at the corner of Broadway and 96th Street, Mark noticed one of the beggars. There was something familiar about the poor soul. Mark walked over to him and said, "Say, don't I know you?"

The man looked up with sunken eyes and quickly looked away. "You must be mistaken," he whispered, shivering in his ragged, heavy overcoat. His face was very thin, and he looked as though he hadn't shaved in weeks.

"Sorry," said Mark.

As he crossed the street, he thought, "I know that guy. That's Bernie Stevens, the teller at the Bank of the United States. The poor guy must be ashamed to be seen in such a state." Mark had often gone into Bernie's bank to cash his paychecks because it was near Wood's. But a little over a year ago, in December 1930, the bank had collapsed. Like other banks all over, it had loaned money to companies that couldn't repay them. "So Bernie hasn't found work in all this time," Mark thought. "That could be me if I don't find a job."

It was dark by the time Mark reached home. Alison took one look at him and her smile turned to a look of alarm. "Mark, what is it? What happened?"

"Wood closed the store," Mark said.

Alison fell into a kitchen chair, her head in her hands. "What are we going to do now?" she cried.

And every week there seemed to be more beggars—men, women, and now children.

Mark hung up his coat and sat down. "Well, I don't think we need to worry yet. We've still got money in the bank." Mark and Alison had been saving money for years at the West Side Bank. "If we have to, we can use our savings to tide us over until I get another job."

For the next few months, Mark spent all his time job hunting, but he had no luck. Every week, he took more money from his savings. And every week there seemed to be more beggars—men, women, and now children.

One cold, sunny day in March, Mark took his kids to Riverside Park. They had not been there in a while. When they got to the corner opposite the park, Mark could hardly believe his eyes.

Sally shouted, "Daddy, what's that?" She pointed at a village of sheds thrown together from packing boxes and scrap metal. Mark had read about similar camps in other parts of the country. Having lost their homes, ordinary citizens built shelters side by side in parks and other public places. People called them "**Hoovervilles**," because they blamed President Hoover for the Depression. Mark couldn't recall the last time anyone had said anything nice about Hoover.

Ordinary citizens built shelters side by side in parks and other public places.

He watched a group of people huddled around a fire for warmth. Then he spotted Bernie Stevens crouching in a large cardboard box. Mark took both of his children's hands in his own. "Listen," said Mark, "those poor people built this camp because they lost their homes. But we have money in the bank, and we will never have to live like this." From then on, Mark avoided the park.

Then, in August 1932, about seven months after Mark lost his job, another disaster struck the

People and Terms to Know

Hoovervilles—communities of sheds, tents, and cars where homeless people lived during the Depression. They were named after the president that many people blamed for their condition.

Murphy family. Mark went to the West Side Bank as usual to withdraw some money. The bank's door was locked with heavy chains. A sign posted on the bank door said "CLOSED." The bank had gone out of business just like any other company. It was hard to understand how this could happen because banks were filled with money! But banks also lend a lot of that money to people and businesses. If these loans are not paid back because people lose jobs and businesses go bust, then the banks run out of money too.

"Oh, no," Mark thought. "I should have paid more attention to what happened to Bernie Stevens and his bank. I could have kept our money in a shoebox! Anything would have been safer than this. Now it's too late. All of our money is gone!"

Sunk in despair, Mark recalled a lone, bold voice promising to do something to turn things around. **Franklin Roosevelt**, the governor of New York, was running against Hoover for president.

People and Terms to Know

Franklin Roosevelt—(1882–1945) 32nd president of the United States, elected first in 1932 and then three times after that. He helped the country get through both the Great Depression and World War II.

▲

In the 1930s a large radio was often the center point of a family's living room.

Roosevelt promised a "new deal" for the American people. But the election was still several months away.

Soon the Murphys, too, joined the long lines waiting for soup and bread. He and Alison struggled to keep their apartment. Things got so bad that they sold most of the family's furniture, clothing, and jewelry. Meanwhile, as Hoover grew even more unpopular, Roosevelt explained how he would create new jobs. On Election Day, American voters dumped Hoover and elected Roosevelt president.

By March 1933, the Murphys still had a home, but it was bare except for their radio, the kitchen table, a few chairs, and their beds. On March 4th, they listened as President Roosevelt gave his **inaugural address** on the radio.

In a firm, confident voice, the new president declared that "the only thing we have to fear is fear itself." He explained how the American people had let fear get in the way of action. Roosevelt promised a "war against the emergency" and told everyone the bold steps he would take to bring the country out of the Depression.

Mark and Alison, along with millions of other Americans, were weary and worn out by the Depression. If this new president, who promised a "new deal," could be so brave, maybe they could be brave too.

People and Terms to Know

inaugural address—speech given by a president at his inauguration, the ceremony in which he is sworn into office.

QUESTIONS TO CONSIDER

1. Why did Mark lose his job?

2. Why wasn't Mark worried when the stock market crashed in 1929?

3. How did President Hoover react to the economic crisis?

4. Why were many banks forced to close during the Depression?

5. In what way did President Roosevelt lift people's spirits when he came into office?

Working for the CCC

BY JUDITH CONAWAY

It was April 7, 1933—my 21st birthday, and the lowest day of my life. I woke up feeling like a total failure. Now, mind you, it wasn't all my fault. The whole United States was deep in the Depression. You don't remember it? Everywhere businesses were failing and factories were closing their doors. There were no jobs. For almost three years I'd been hungry pretty much all the time. There's no other way to say it. And there were millions of others as bad off as I was.

Franklin Roosevelt had become president only a month earlier. During the election he had promised "a new deal for the American people," but I didn't put much stock in the promises of politicians. At

CCC boys working in 1935 at a U.S. Department of Agriculture research center in Maryland.

this point the **New Deal** had barely begun. But I'd been living on the road for a long time, and I sure didn't see anything new out there.

I drifted from town to town, looking for work wherever I could find it—Virginia, West Virginia, Maryland. I wasn't picky. I just wanted to be close enough to my hometown so that if something really bad happened (though I don't know how things could have gotten worse), my family wouldn't be too far away. Most of the time I stayed away because I didn't know how to make life on the farm any better. My family was on **relief**. The last thing they needed was another mouth to feed.

I drifted from town to town, looking for work wherever I could find it.

Every year on my birthday, though, I made a point of going back home. It's not like there would be a cake or anything. It was just good to see everyone, and maybe have a cup of coffee that I didn't have to worry about paying for. But this year was different. I was a man now and ashamed that I still

People and Terms to Know

New Deal—series of federal government programs designed to reverse the economic depression of the 1930s and to relieve poverty.

relief—general name for the mixture of private, state, and federal programs that provide help to the poor.

couldn't help my family. Also, if I went home, I'd be given food that otherwise would go to my little brothers and sisters. I guess I could have refused the food, but I didn't trust my hunger to let me say no to it.

No, I was determined not to return home unless I had money in my pocket. But the chances of making money that morning seemed about as good as *me* getting elected president. Thinking about all this on my birthday brought me to a low, low point.

I'd spent the night in a barn and had to move before the farmer came out to milk the cows. I took a very cold bath in a nearby creek. It was still dark. Then I walked three miles to the nearest town.

I reached the town square as the sky was starting to get light. The only place open was a diner. In fact, it looked like the only place that hadn't gone out of business. I could see a beautiful girl inside, mopping the floor. I tapped on the door politely, glad that I had taken that bath.

"I'll be happy to mop that floor for you, Miss, in return for a cup of coffee," I said, with my best smile.

I finished mopping while Emily (that was the girl's name) got busy in the kitchen. Before I knew it, I was sitting in a booth, eating biscuits and gravy. Emily even brought me the morning paper.

There it was—my lucky headline: "Government Will Hire Local Youths." The article was about a new program from President Roosevelt. The **Civilian Conservation Corps** was hiring unmarried men ages 18 to 25 whose families were on relief. It sounded like outdoor work, the kind I'm good at. Hiring would begin that very day—

> *I wasn't worried about the competition. I just knew my luck had changed at last.*

at an address right across the town square! I jumped up, gave Emily a big kiss, and dashed out the door.

I was the very first guy in line. By the time that government office opened, there were dozens of other young men behind me. But I wasn't worried about the competition. I just knew my luck had changed at last.

I was 100 percent right. And so I proudly joined "Roosevelt's Tree Army." Between 1933 and 1942, about three million men like me worked for the

Civilian Conservation Corps. I stayed in for the full two years. Those years were what really changed me from a boy into a man, not turning 21.

We'd been hungry and homeless for weeks and months at a time.

In the CCC, they put us into work camps run by the army. We slept in tents or **barracks**—up to thirty guys in one room. We used outdoor **latrines** and showers. We ate army food and dressed in army clothes. It doesn't sound like much fun, does it? But we all thought we'd died and gone to heaven.

You've got to understand where we were coming from. We'd been hungry and homeless for weeks and months at a time. Then, suddenly, we had three full meals a day. We had a warm, dry place to sleep and new clothes. We even had medical and dental care.

Best of all, we had real jobs. We didn't have to take handouts from the government. The pay was $30 a month, $25 of which went to our families. That might not seem like a lot of money for a month's work, but remember we also got food,

---

People and Terms to Know

barracks—sleeping quarters for soldiers.
latrines—toilets.

clothing, and shelter. Even so, $5 a month for spending money doesn't sound like much, does it? But in those days a candy bar cost a nickel, and going to the movies cost a dime. To have more than a dollar a week to spend on yourself—why, that was striking it rich!

I can't tell you how proud I was to be sending that money home. My CCC money helped save our family farm! My folks could put meat on the table once in a while. Mom got a new dress for church. I was a hero to my brothers and sisters. When I visited the farm, which was more often now, I brought flowers and candy and everyone acted like I was Santa Claus.

When us CCC guys weren't working hard, we were playing hard. We had a camp band and practiced whenever we could. On weekends we played baseball against men from other camps. We even organized a picnic and invited girls from the surrounding towns. I invited Emily. We'd been writing letters to each other for a while now, but this was the first time we'd seen each other since the day we met.

We ate chicken and corn and then snuck away from the picnic and went up a path that I knew. We

▲

Although CCC employment was limited to young men, young women also did conservation projects for the government. Here, young women work at a U.S. Department of Agriculture timber salvage sawmill.

walked for about half an hour, but she didn't complain. Suddenly the trees in front of us stopped, and there seemed to be only sky in front of us. Then Emily realized that we were on top of a mountain looking down into a green valley.

"This is my favorite place on Earth," I said. "Isn't this an amazing view?"

She smiled. "Yes, it is. And you're responsible for it."

"What do you mean? Only God can take credit for something this beautiful." She really had me confused.

"Yes, the valley was already here," she said. "But you helped make it so that people could enjoy the view. Didn't you say that you helped clear that trail back there? And didn't you build up a mound of dirt to keep that creek from flooding in the spring?"

"In other words," I laughed, "I cleaned the place up."

"Exactly," she said. "And I seem to remember that you're good at cleaning things up."

She was reminding me of how I mopped the floor on our first "date." Now we were both laughing.

I'm worried that it sounds like I'm saying life in the CCC was a bed of roses. No, it was very hard work. Most of it was outdoor work like digging ditches, shoveling dirt, and building walls. We put in a full forty-hour week. What with eating regularly and getting all that exercise, we gained weight and put on muscle.

I was in one of the very first work camps. We worked right in **Shenandoah National Park**. We

People and Terms to Know

Shenandoah National Park—forest of almost 200,000 acres located along the top of the Blue Ridge Mountains in northern Virginia.

Working for the CCC 175

did all kinds of different jobs, from planting trees to building cabins to clearing hiking trails.

The hardest work we did was on a beautiful road called Skyline Drive. When we started, the road was a mess. Big chunks of pavement had broken off. We filled in the holes and widened the road. Then, to make it even safer, we built walls to hold the sides of the road in place. We planted trees and bushes to help control **erosion**.

We also built scenic overlooks at the most beautiful spots along the road. I remember the day we opened part of the road to the public. We had an open house at the camp, and of course I invited Emily. We climbed into the camp trucks and drove up to my favorite overlook. "At least now we don't have to walk all the way to enjoy the view," she said.

When we were alone and looking out over the trees and clouds, I asked her to marry me. She said, "It's a deal."

So now you know why my twenty-first birthday was the luckiest day of my life. On that day, I

People and Terms to Know

erosion—wearing away of land due to flooding, wind, or other natural causes.

ate my first breakfast in three weeks and I got my first job in three years. And I met the girl who later became my wife. Of course that meant I could no longer work for the CCC, which was for single men only. But I didn't mind. I got a job working in the diner.

By the way, the very first deal Emily and I made is still on. She makes breakfast, and I mop the kitchen floor.

QUESTIONS TO CONSIDER

1. What problems did people in the countryside have during the Great Depression?

2. What was the New Deal?

3. How did the Civilian Conservation Corps improve people's lives?

4. What in your opinion was the hardest part of the narrator's life as a young man during the Depression?

Surviving the Dust Bowl

BY JUDITH LLOYD YERO

On old maps, it was called the "Great American Desert"—a flat, treeless land where the wind blew all the time. But in the 1920s, as the demand for wheat increased, prices rose because farmers could charge more and still have buyers. Thousands of farmers rushed to the Southern Plains states such as Oklahoma, eager to make money.

They saw healthy, green land covered in natural grasses but ignored the high winds. They thought that the farming methods they'd used in the Northeast would work anywhere. Their steel plows cut into the heavy **sod**, exposing rich soil that "looked like chocolate."

People and Terms to Know

sod—surface layer of soil covered with grasses.

Wind-blown dust darkens the sky in Amarillo, Texas.

Tractors swarmed like insects over 100 million acres of the southwestern plains, breaking up land that had never known the plow. Farmers planted the tilled land with winter wheat. One of them, Lawrence Svobida, later wrote, "I believe any man must see beauty in mile upon mile of level land where the wheat, waist high, bends in the slightest breeze and turns a golden yellow under a flaming July sun. To me it is breathtaking, the most beautiful scene in all the world."

With dreams of making money fast, even eastern businessmen bought land, planted crops, and went home until it was time to harvest. They were called "suitcase farmers."

"The rain will follow the plow," the farmers said hopefully. And it did—until the 1930s. A farmer named J. R. Davison remembered the late 1920s like this: "I think that most of those who came to this part of the country thought it was just 'hog heaven.' You know, it'll always be this way. So they kept breaking this land out, and they plowed up a lot of country that should never have been plowed up."

The problem was that these farmers did not understand that they had arrived during one small moment when the land was healthy. They didn't know that for long periods there was no rain at all, a situation that had given the region its name on those old maps.

Suddenly the rains stopped, not for days or weeks, but for years. The crops dried up. The soil, its natural covering of heavy grasses gone, turned to dust. In 1931, the "black blizzards" began. The over-plowed and **over-grazed** soil,

They didn't know that for long periods there was no rain at all.

carried by the ever-present winds, blew away with the dreams of the farmers. Millions of tons of swirling dust filled the air. It had taken a thousand years to build an inch of **topsoil** on the Southern Plains, but only minutes for the wind to carry it all away.

Everything the farmers had worked for was gone. The fine dust was everywhere—in their food, in their beds, and in the lungs of many who would never recover. After traveling through the area, one writer called it the **Dust Bowl**.

People and Terms to Know

over-grazed—referring to land that has had its plant life eaten away by livestock such as cattle and sheep.

topsoil—surface soil of land, necessary for farming.

Dust Bowl—area of the American plains where poor farming methods and dry weather led to the wind carrying away millions of acres of soil in the 1930s.

*   *   *

Many families gave up and left for places like California, where they hoped they could rebuild their lives. But most families stayed. Their stories are told by the survivors.

"The farmhouses looked terrible—the dust was deposited clear up to the window sills in these farmhouses. Even about half of the front door was blocked by this sand. And if people inside wanted to get out, they had to climb out through the window to shovel out the front door. And there was no longer any yard at all there, not a green sprig, not a living thing of any kind, not even a field mouse. Nothing." —Judge Cowen

"The angry winds had strength beyond my wildest imagination. They blew continuously for a hundred hours, and it seemed as if the whole surface of the earth would be blown away. As far as my eyes could see, my fields were completely bare." —Lawrence Svobida

"It kept gittin' worse and worse and wind blowin' harder and harder and it kept gittin' darker and darker. And the old house was just a-vibratin' like it was gonna blow away. And I started tryin' to see my hand. And I kept bringin' my hand up

▲
An Oklahoma farmer and his sons flee from a dust storm.

closer and closer and closer and closer and I finally touched the end of my nose and I still couldn't see my hand. That's how black it was." —Melt White

"Our parents had to turn the plates upside-down on the tables and cover 'em with a sheet. Babies had to sleep with wet sheets over their cribs

so that they wouldn't breathe all that dirt."
—Imogene Glover

"Birds flew in terror before the storm, and only those with strong wings escaped. The smaller birds became exhausted, then fell to the ground, to share the fate of the thousands of jackrabbits that died from suffocation."
—Lawrence Svobida

> *"Birds flew in terror before the storm, and only those with strong wings escaped."*

"We always went to the cellar when there was a bad dust storm coming, 'cause the first bad, bad one that I remember, we didn't know if our house would blow away! And my daddy took the hoe and ax and a scoop to the cellar with us. I know that he took the ax in case dust covered up the door, and he had to break the wood in the cellar door to get us out. Then he needed the scoop to scoop the dirt out. The only reason I think that he took the hoe was because it had the longest handle and he could poke it up through the vent in the ceiling of the cellar to be sure that we were getting air. One time I didn't quite get back to the cellar before the dirt hit and I can remember that it burned." —Imogene Glover

* * *

Even as the dust blew and the rain continued to stay away, many farmers could not believe that these terrible conditions would last.

"A lot of different thoughts and ideas went through people's mind. Some people thought it was an act of God . . . a punishment . . . and possibly in a way it kindly was, because they'd been careless and wounded the land. God didn't create the plains to be farmland. He created it for what He put on it, in grass and cattle. And they come in and completely changed it. They abused it somethin' terrible. They got everything out they could."
—Melt White

In 1939, the rains finally came. For many, it was too late. "With my money completely gone, and my health not far behind it, I was at last ready to admit defeat and leave the Dust Bowl forever. With youth and ambition ground into the very dust itself, I could only drift with the tide." —Lawrence Svobida

Others were hopeful about the future. "When the rain came, it meant life itself. It meant a future. It meant that there would be something better ahead. You didn't have false hope any more, you knew then that you was going to have some crops."
—Floyd Coen

Farmers had been forced to accept the limits of the land and to think differently about taking care of it. But some still wondered whether anything had really changed. Even today many people wonder if our farming methods are examples of **sustainable agriculture**.

"Don't fool yourself. You can't convince me we've learned our lesson. It's just not in our blood to play a safe game." —Melt White

QUESTIONS TO CONSIDER

1. Why did so many farmers move to the southwestern plains?

2. Why were the farmers wrong in assuming that farming practices they had used in the Northeast would work anywhere?

3. How do you think the dust storms would have affected the lives of the people?

4. What kinds of activities are humans doing today that might cause problems like the Dust Bowl?

People and Terms to Know

sustainable agriculture—farming that respects and protects the land so that future farmers can use it as well.

Children of the Dust Bowl: The True Story of the School at Weedpatch Camp
by Jerry Stanley

Jerry Stanley has brought together letters and interviews to show how children were affected by the Dust Bowl. Life was difficult for these kids, and yet they found ways to survive and go to school.

Treasures in the Dust
by Tracey Porter

Annie and Violet are best friends. Annie stays on her family's farm in Oklahoma during the Dust Bowl, but Violet moves with her family to California. There she finds herself working in the fields. This is an emotional story of the hard times of the Dust Bowl.

Driven From the Land: The Story of the Dust Bowl
by Milton Meltzer

This is a nonfiction book that gives a detailed history of the Dust Bowl. The families who moved from their farms on the plains were part of a larger movement of families during those years. This book shows the "big picture" of the Dust Bowl.

Dorothea Lange Records the Depression

BY MARY KATHLEEN FLYNN

Dorothea Lange's photographs of farm families in the 1930s prove the expression, "a picture is worth a thousand words." Each photograph tells a moving story of the poverty and despair Americans faced throughout the decade. Poor harvests, **drought**, dust storms, and the stock market crash of 1929 all contributed to the Great Depression.

Dorothea Lange began her career in the 1920s. At first, she made portraits for paying customers. Then the good times of the 1920s gave way to the hard times of the 1930s. Lange grew tired of studio work and took her camera to the streets. The work

People and Terms to Know

drought—long period of dry weather.
Dorothea Lange—(1895–1965) famous photographer of the American people during the 1930s.

Lange's *White Angel Breadline* shows men waiting for food from a charity.

she did there and in country roads across America made her famous. Some of her photos during this period appear here, along with Lange's thoughts about them.

The country's economy got better in the early 1940s. But Dorothea Lange continued to photograph people in difficult situations until her death in 1965. The following year, her husband gave her collection of original photographs to the Oakland Museum of California. Since Lange took her photographs of the Depression as part of one of the government programs, they are now property of the United States. That means they belong to all of us, which only seems right.

One of Lange's early street photographs is called *White Angel Breadline*. It was taken in San Francisco in 1932. In many ways, 1932 was the worst time in the Depression. It was before Franklin Roosevelt became president in 1933 and started the programs that gave jobs—and hope—to people.

The photograph shows a man with a hat pulled over his eyes. His mouth is just a straight line without expression. His hands are folded tightly in front of him. Behind him is a sea of other men in hats who seem no better off than he is. As the man leans forward on a wooden railing, he holds a tin cup between his elbows. The cup is empty. Anyone who looks at this photograph can sense the emptiness and sadness at the heart of the Depression.

"I made that [photograph] on the first day I ever went in an area where people said, 'Oh, don't go there.' It was on the first day that I ever made a photograph actually on the street."

Anyone who looks at this photograph can sense the emptiness and sadness at the heart of the Depression.

Another photo from this period (1934) also deals with the feeling of emptiness, of having nothing. It shows a man hugging his head on his knees. The only other thing in the photo is an upside-down wheelbarrow, which is why the title is *Man Beside Wheelbarrow*. You can tell that the wheelbarrow must be empty to be turned upside-down like that.

There are no other signs of human life in the photo—no people in the background, not even any writing on the wall. And because we cannot see his eyes, the man does not even connect with us. He is truly alone.

▲

Man Beside Wheelbarrow

"*I wanted to take a picture of a man as he stood in his world—in this case, a man with his head down, with his back against the wall, with his __livelihood__, like the wheelbarrow, overturned.*"

Lange's photos of people on the streets of San Francisco led to her being hired by the government

---

People and Terms to Know

livelihood—way of making a living.

---

in 1935. Her job was to record the lives of **migrant workers** for the Farm Security Administration. Many of these workers had been field workers who moved to California to find new work after their farms had failed.

Perhaps Lange's most famous photo is *Migrant Mother*. It shows a woman cupping her chin with her hand. Her eyebrows are drawn together, and her mouth is pulled into a frown. She looks off in

Migrant Mother ▶

People and Terms to Know

migrant workers—people who move from place to place in order to find work.

the distance. Maybe she's watching something, or maybe she's watching *for* something. There are children clinging to her. One child is asleep on her lap. Another leans on her shoulder, possibly sleeping. A third child is leaning on her other shoulder, possibly crying. The year is 1936.

> *Maybe she's watching something, or maybe she's watching for something.*

"*I saw and approached the hungry and desperate mother, as if drawn by a magnet. I do not remember how I explained my presence or my camera to her, but I do remember she asked me no questions. . . . She told me her age, that she was 32. She said that they had been living on frozen vegetables from the surrounding fields and birds that the children killed. She had just sold the tires from her car to buy food. There she sat in that lean-to tent with her children huddled around her, and seemed to know that my pictures might help her, and so she helped me. There was a sort of equality about it.*"

Many of the families who appear in Lange's photos were fleeing from the Dust Bowl. That's what they called the high plains of Texas, Oklahoma, New Mexico, Colorado, and Kansas. A long drought was followed by strong winds. The

▲

Oklahoma Drought Refugees

result was that huge dust storms blew through the area. They wiped out farms and damaged farm equipment. In 1938, farmers lost about 850 million tons of topsoil.

The families who had hoped to find a better life in California instead found themselves living out of their cars or camped out in tents. One such family is the subject of Lange's 1935 photo *Oklahoma Drought **Refugees***. A man stands in an empty field

People and Terms to Know

Refugees—people who flee a terrible situation such as war or drought in search of safety, or *refuge*.

in front of some tents and a car. In the background, a woman stands in front of one of the tents, looking at him uncertainly. What is she thinking?

"Their roots were all torn out. The only background they had was a background of utter poverty. It's very hard to photograph a proud man against a background like that, because it doesn't show what he's proud about. I had to get my camera to register the things about these people that were more important than how poor they were—their pride, their strength, their spirit."

In a photo called *Family on the Road*, a man, a woman, four children, and a dog stand beside their car. It is piled high with their belongings, including furniture. It is hard to imagine a car traveling very far while carrying such a big load. It

▲
Family on the Road

is also hard to imagine a family loaded down with so much trouble.

But it is easy to look at this photograph and become worried about the family. For instance, what do you think might happen to them if the car broke down?

"I looked at the license plate on the car and it was Oklahoma. I got out and asked which way were they going. . . . And they said, 'We've been blown out. . . .' They were the first arrivals that I saw. These were the people who got up that day quick and left. They saw they had no crop back there. They had to get out."

"I got out and asked which way were they going. . . . And they said, 'We've been blown out. . . .'"

Lange saw enormous changes in the way farmers lived their lives. One of these was the introduction of equipment that was bigger and more powerful. That meant it took fewer people to work a farm. Farming also required different skills. Now farmers had to know how to use complex machines instead of just using an animal, such as a mule, for the same job. With all of these changes to farming, and the many bad years of the 1930s, it's no wonder that many farmers and their children moved to cities.

Man on Farm-All Tractor

In another 1938 photo, *Man on Farm-All Tractor*, a man sits on top of a large tractor. In a way, he is as alone as the man we saw earlier in *Man beside Wheelbarrow*.

"There is no place for people to go to live on the land anymore, and they're living. That's a wild statement, isn't it? And yet, it begins to look as though it's true in

our country. We have, in my lifetime, changed from __rural__ *to* __urban__. *In my lifetime, that little space, this tremendous thing has happened."*

QUESTIONS TO CONSIDER

1. Why is a picture "worth a thousand words"?
2. What were some of the causes of the Great Depression?
3. How do Dorothea Lange's photographs make you feel?
4. How might Dorothea Lange's photographs have helped someone like the woman in *Migrant Mother*?
5. What did Lange mean when she said that it was a "tremendous thing" when Americans changed from rural to urban people?

People and Terms to Know

rural—country-like.
urban—city-like.

The Martians Invade

BY FITZGERALD HIGGINS

I can remember the whole crazy event like it was yesterday, although now it's a lifetime ago. It took place on October 30, 1938. To understand what happened, you have to know those were nervous days for all of us.

It was just before **World War II** broke out. Most of the news reports coming over the radio were bad. In Europe and the Far East, armies were marching. There were rumors of terrible new weapons that could make this war worse than before. I was only 8 years old at the time and didn't understand much of

---

People and Terms to Know

World War II—(1939–1945) war between the Axis powers (Germany, Italy, and Japan) and the Allies (England, the Soviet Union, France, China, and the United States). It broke out September 1, 1939, when Germany invaded Poland, and ended with the surrender of Germany and Japan in 1945.

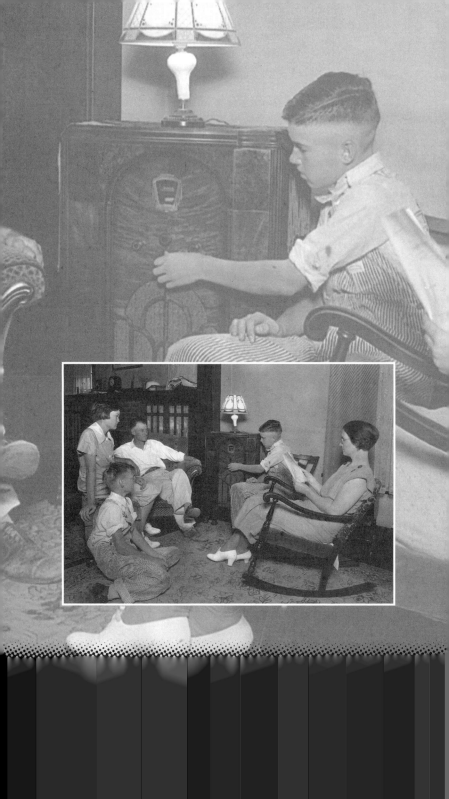

what was going on. However, I watched my parents' worried faces as they listened to the news, and I could tell things weren't going well.

It all began at eight o'clock Sunday evening. As usual, my family was gathered around the radio. Dad was sitting in his worn armchair. Mom was in her rocker with the new baby on her lap. My sister and I were lying on the floor, working on a jigsaw puzzle. We had been listening, like we usually did at that time, to the **Edgar Bergen-Charlie McCarthy program**. But then, about ten minutes into the show, this girl singer came on, and we decided to change channels.

Mom leaned over and turned the dial. All of a sudden, we heard an excited voice saying, "—half buried in a vast pit. Must have struck with terrific force. The ground is covered with splinters of a tree it must have struck on its way down." Mom was about to switch to another station, when Dad said, "Wait a sec, honey, let's hear what he's talking about."

It sounded like a news report. A reporter was at a place in New Jersey called Grover's Mill, about 20

People and Terms to Know

Edgar Bergen-Charlie McCarthy program—popular radio program featuring ventriloquist Edgar Bergen (1903–1978) and his dummy Charlie McCarthy. It was America's most popular radio program in 1938.

miles from **Trenton**. I'd never heard of it, but we live in eastern Pennsylvania, so we weren't too far away. Something strange had fallen from the sky and slammed into a farmer's field there. The reporter said there were hundreds of people gathered around the pit the thing had made when it crashed. The reporter's voice

> *Something strange had fallen from the sky and slammed into a farmer's field there.*

just kept getting more and more upset as he described what happened next.

Weird creatures crawled slowly out of the pit. They were like big, flabby spiders. Some policemen walked toward them with a white handkerchief tied to a pole. Over the radio you could hear this awful hissing, humming sound. The creatures in the pit shot a jet of flame at the policemen and set them on fire! Then they set the whole surrounding field on fire!

There was the sound of explosions as cars blew up. The reporter screamed, "—it's spreading everywhere. It's coming this way. About twenty yards to my right—" There was a crash and then silence.

People and Terms to Know

Trenton—capital of New Jersey, located in the west central part of the state, on its border with Pennsylvania.

We all sat and looked at each other. I noticed Mom was hugging the baby tightly to her. She spoke very quietly to Dad, as if she was trying to keep any fear out of her voice. "What do think has happened, Jim? You don't think it's . . . ?" She didn't finish her question. Maybe she didn't want to frighten us kids. Or maybe she just wasn't sure *how* to finish her question.

"I'm not sure what's happening, dear," Dad answered. "But let's keep our heads. What's the radio saying now?" We kept listening, and the reports kept getting worse. Forty people had been burned to a crisp in the farmer's field! They interviewed a scientist who had been there. He said the creatures had used some sort of heat ray.

He wouldn't say where he thought the creatures were from or why they had come to Earth.

Parts of New Jersey were placed under **martial law**. Seven thousand troops were called out to surround the creatures. The battle was over practically before it began. Only 120 of the soldiers

People and Terms to Know

martial (MAHR•shuhl) **law**—military rule of a country or other region in time of war or emergency.

survived. Now the radio announcer gave the grim answer to my Mom's question. The creatures in the pit were the advance guard of an invading army from Mars!

Dad got up and went to the window. He looked up at the night sky, as if he were searching for the next wave of attackers. I joined him at the window and looked up our little street. Doors were opening and people were coming out. Some stood staring up at the sky like my Dad. Others gathered in small groups and talked. I could see people pointing up at the stars and down toward the distant lights of the city in the valley below us.

The Secretary of the Interior spoke from Washington. He urged us to place our faith in God and the army.

News kept coming in. The **Secretary of the Interior** spoke from Washington. He urged us to place our faith in God and the army. There were reports of a second and third Martian landing. The Martians had put war machines together that were

People and Terms to Know

Secretary of the Interior—U.S. government official in charge of public lands who reports to the president.

moving across the countryside at great speed. Their goal was clearly to reach nearby New York City. Eight army bombers tried to stop them but were destroyed by the Martian heat rays. There was panic in New York as people awaited the arrival of the invaders.

At this point, the phone rang. I think we all jumped. Dad walked over and picked up the receiver. It was his sister, I recall. He asked Mom to turn down the radio for a moment so he could hear better.

"Don't you think we should keep listening, dear?" Mom asked nervously. "Tell whoever it is you'll call them back."

"It's Jane!" Dad hissed back at her in an annoyed tone, holding his hand over the receiver. "You know I can't tell her that. She sounds terrified!"

"She usually does," my sister muttered.

My aunt Jane was always pretty nervous. If she would hear a story about a house that had been robbed three towns over, she'd look under all of the beds. I couldn't imagine what the threat of a Martian invasion would do to her. One word from her big brother might have made her shoo her family into their old Ford and head for the hills.

"Now, Jane," we heard Dad say. It was clear he was trying to keep her calm. "I don't want you doing anything until we have more information."

I was still standing at the window. The neighbors weren't looking at the sky anymore. They were carrying suitcases, cardboard boxes full of food, and blankets. They packed all this in their cars, got in with their kids, and drove off down the street. Looking down the hill, I could see that the highway that led out of the city was full of traffic. Everyone had the same idea—to get away from where they thought the Martians would attack next. But nobody knew where that would be!

We returned to the radio, where the scientist who had escaped from the scene of the first Martian attack was talking to some other survivors. Listening to them, Dad's worried look gave way to puzzlement. Turning to Mom, he said, "You know, dear, I'm beginning to wonder about all this. This doesn't sound like a news program anymore. It sounds like a play. And now that I think about it, everything happened too fast. How could the army show up in the middle of New Jersey in a few minutes?"

▲

Orson Welles rehearses a radio program.

Mother agreed, and that's why we didn't join our neighbors in fleeing. In fact, my sister and I were calmly working on the jigsaw puzzle again when **Orson Welles** came on the radio. He announced that the broadcast had all been just a Halloween prank. Later I found out from a friend that if we had listened more carefully we would have known this earlier on. But then I figured out that this moment had come when my aunt telephoned and we couldn't hear the radio!

People and Terms to Know

Orson Welles—(1915–1985) American filmmaker and actor. He became nationally famous as a result of "The War of the Worlds" broadcast. He next went to Hollywood, where he directed and starred in *Citizen Kane* (1941).

*   *   *

The next day, a lot of people didn't think Welles's prank had been too funny. The night before, there had been panic as many Americans became convinced that the world was coming to an end. Welles had to make a public apology for scaring America silly.

Many people looked for explanations for what had happened. One **sociologist** joked that the panic took place because all the intelligent people were listening to the dummy Charlie McCarthy instead of **"The War of the Worlds."** But other people saw a serious lesson in the event. They felt it showed the dangerous power of radio when it was becoming the main source of information for most Americans.

QUESTIONS TO CONSIDER

1. According to the narrator, how did the situation overseas help make people believe that the United States was being invaded?

2. How was the radio program "The War of the Worlds" presented?

3. What does "The War of the Worlds" broadcast show about the power of radio in 1938?

4. What do you think the American people should have learned from this experience?

People and Terms to Know

"The War of the Worlds"—originally a science fiction book by English writer H. G. Wells in which Martians invade earth. Orson Welles changed the story for radio by making it up-to-date and setting it in New Jersey.

Report of the Panic

On October 31, 1938, *The New York Times* reported the panic that had been caused by the "War of the Worlds" broadcast the night before.

A wave of mass hysteria seized thousands of radio listeners between 8:15 and 9:30 o'clock last night when a broadcast of a dramatization of H. G. Wells's fantasy, "The War of the Worlds," led thousands to believe that an interplanetary conflict had started with invading Martians spreading wide death and destruction in New Jersey and New York.

The broadcast, which disrupted households, interrupted religious services, created traffic jams and clogged communications systems, was made by Orson Welles, who as the radio character, "The Shadow," used to give "the creeps" to countless child listeners. This time at least a score of adults required medical treatment for shock and hysteria.

In Newark, in a single block at Heddon Terrace and Hawthorne Avenue, more than twenty families rushed out of their houses with wet handkerchiefs and towels over their faces to flee from what they believed was to be a gas raid. Some began moving household furniture.

Throughout New York families left their homes, some to flee to near-by parks. Thousands of persons called the police, newspapers and radio stations here and in other cities of the United States and Canada seeking advice on protective measures against the raids.

Sources

Jeannette Rankin Votes No *by Judith Lloyd Yero*

As the first woman in Congress, Jeannette Rankin's words and actions were recorded in many places. The sections of the story that describe her anti-war philosophy are taken from an interview that Miss Rankin gave to John Board in 1965. A good general biography of Jeannette Rankin is *Flight of the Dove: The Story of Jeannette Rankin* by Kevin S. Giles (Beaverton, OR: The Touchstone Press, 1980).

Moving Toward the Promised Land *by Marianne McComb*

Selena and her family are fictional characters, although the newspaper that they read, *The Defender*, really did exist. It played a key role in urging African Americans to leave the South and migrate North during the 1920s. A strong overview of the period is provided in *Bound for the Promised Land* by Michael L. Cooper (Lodestar Books: 1995).

Sergeant York Captures a "Few" Germans
by Walter Hazen

Alvin York, Sergeant Early, Lieutenant Woods, and General Lindsay are historical figures. Only the narrator is fictional. The words spoken by York in the story are taken directly from his autobiography, *Sergeant York: His Own Life and War Diary* by Alvin C. York and edited by Tom Skeyhill (New York: Doubleday, Doran and Co., 1928). For readers interested in World War I, the author recommends Zachary Kent's *World War I: "The War to End Wars."* (Hillside, NJ: Enslow Publishers, Inc., 1994).

An American Nurse Cares for the Wounded *by Jane Leder*

The narrator, Jenny Carter, as well as her classmates, such as Bobby Carlson, are fictional. The major historical source for this story is Shirley Millard's *I Saw Them Die* (New York: Harcourt, Brace and Company, 1936). This gripping first-person account of what life was like in a World War I hospital is highly recommended. For readers interested in online information about the battles and events of the Great War, public broadcasting's web site (www.pbs.org) includes a timeline and other features.

Surviving the Flu Epidemic *by Mary Kathleen Flynn*

Dr. Stern is a fictional character, but Dr. Vaughan and the main events described at Camp Devens and Camp Funston are real. Dr. Vaughan visited Camp Devens in September 1918. An excellent portrayal of the devastating epidemic can be found in the documentary "The American Experience: Influenza 1918." Information about this PBS film may be available online at www.pbs.org.

Cars for the People *by Stephen Currie*

The characters in the story are all fictional, although the fascinating founder of the Ford Motor Company, Henry Ford, has been the subject of countless books. A good one is *Ford: The Men and the Machine* by Robert Lacey (Boston: Little, Brown, 1986). For facts relating to what it was like to work for Ford, the author of this story used *Ford: The Wayward Capitalist* by Carol Gelderman (New York: Dial, 1981), a lively account of Ford's many triumphs and setbacks.

Bernice Talks to Mother *by Dee Masters*

The original short story "Bernice Bobs Her Hair" by F. Scott Fitzgerald can be found in many short story collections, including *The Bodley Head Scott Fitzgerald Short Stories* (London: The Bodley Head, 1963). The author also used the following magazine sources for details on the flappers of the period: "Flapper Jane" by Bruce Bliven in *The New Republic*, September 9, 1925; "A Flapper's Appeal To Parents" by Ellen Welles Page in *Outlook*, December 6, 1922.

A Writer Comes to Harlem *by Marianne McComb*

The narrator of this story, and her grandmother, Louisa P. Jackson, are fictional characters. The people Louisa P. Jackson met, including Jessie Redmon Fauset, Langston Hughes, Zora Neale Hurston, and Claude McKay are historical figures. They all played important roles in the literary and artistic revolution that was the Harlem Renaissance. For more information on such personalities as these, readers might be interested in the book *Extraordinary People of the Harlem Renaissance* by P. Stephen Hardy and Sheila Jackson Hardy (Grolier Publishing, 2000).

The Scopes Trial *by Danny Miller*

The characters of Charlene, her family, and her friend Wanda are fictional. Five days after the Scopes Trial ended, William Jennings Bryan died in his sleep. Clarence Darrow appealed the case to the Tennessee Supreme Court and the verdict was eventually overturned. Even so, the anti-evolution law stayed on the Tennessee books for another 40 years. To learn more about this controversial case, see the Pulitzer Prize-winning book *Summer for the Gods: The Scopes Trial and American's Continuing Debate Over Science and Religion* by Edward J. Larson (HarperCollins Publishers, 1997).

Lindbergh *by Brian J. Mahoney*

The narrator, her brother Jimmy, and her boyfriend Ralph are fictional characters. This story is based on real events following the historic flight of Charles Lindbergh. Lindbergh became an international hero after his daring flight, and he went on to pioneer many new international air routes. Later, however, his baby would be kidnapped and murdered in an affair that shocked America to its core. You can learn more about Lindbergh in *Lindbergh* (G. P. Putnam and Sons, 1963) and from Lindbergh's own account that won him the Pulitzer Prize, *The Spirit of St. Louis* (Charles Scribner's Sons, 1953).

"The Only Thing We Have to Fear Is Fear Itself"
by Stephen Feinstein

The characters in this story—the Murphy family, Mr. Wood, Bernie Stevens—are all fictional. The text of Franklin D. Roosevelt's famous speech, as well as other details of what life was like in this period, can be found in T. H. Watkins's *The Great Depression: America in the 1930s* (Little, Brown and Company, 1993). Another solid source used by the author was *Franklin D. Roosevelt and the New Deal: 1932–1940* by William E. Leuchtenburg (Harper & Row, Publishers, 1963).

Working for the CCC
by Judith Conaway

The narrator and all other characters are fictional. But the Civilian Conservation Corps was an actual government program, the results of whose work we still enjoy in national parks throughout the United States. The National Park Service web site has excellent online information, including a history of the CCC, at www.cr.nps.gov. Two publications from this government agency were also used: "Shenandoah: A Historical Overview" by Reed Engle and John C. Paige's *Eyewitness: The Civilian Conservation Corps and the National Park Service, 1933–1942: An Administrative History*. The author also used a testimonial from Keith Hufford, a former CCC enrollee, from the National Archives and Records Administration's "Success Stories."

Surviving the Dust Bowl *by Judith Lloyd Yero*

All of the people named in the story are real and their quotations are accurate. An excellent source of information on the Dust Bowl is *The American Experience*, a program produced by PBS. At the PBS web site (www.pbs.org), you can find the complete stories told by many of the people who survived the dust storms of the 1930s.

Dorothea Lange Records the Depression
by Mary Kathleen Flynn

A terrific overview of Lange's life and work can be found in *Dorothea Lange: A Visual Life* by Elizabeth Partridge (Smithsonian Institution Press, 1994). Lange's photographs, as well biographical information about her, are also widely available on government web sites. The author used *The Great Depression: America in the 1930s*, by T. H. Watkins, (Little, Brown, 1993) as a source of details for the period.

The Martians Invade *by Fitzgerald Higgins*

The narrator and his family are fictional. The 1938 broadcast of *War of the Worlds* and the resulting panic are historical. The principal source for this story is Howard Koch's *The Panic Broadcast: Portrait of an Event*. Koch was the young scriptwriter who created the radio adaptation of the *War of the Worlds* for Orson Welles' Mercury Theatre. His account, which includes the complete script of the radio play, describes the events leading up to the broadcast on October 30, 1938, and the chaos that resulted.

Glossary of People and Terms to Know

ACLU—American Civil Liberties Union, a group that works to protect the individual rights and liberties guaranteed by the Constitution and laws of the United States. It provides lawyers free of charge to defend people accused of breaking laws it believes are unconstitutional and to help people go to court when their rights have been violated.

"Ain't We Got Fun"—popular song of the 1920s.

alliances—agreements among groups of nations or people to support one another or work together toward a common goal.

Argonne Forest—forest in northeast France that was the site of an important World War I battle.

assembly line—arrangement in which products are put together in stages as they pass from worker to worker or machine to machine, often on a conveyor belt.

autopsy—examination of a dead body to learn the cause of death.

barnstormer—early stunt flyer who performed wild flying tricks.

barracks—sleeping quarters for soldiers.

Belleau (beh•LOH) **Wood**—forest near the Marne River that was well defended by German forces in World War I. The French commander ordered American soldiers to retake it, which they did—at great cost.

blues—raw, emotional kind of music started in the South by African Americans and later developed in the North in cities like Chicago.

bobbed—referring to women's hair cut very short (as short as a man's in back) with bangs, and longer hair on the sides around the face.

boll weevil—small, grayish, long-snouted beetle that lays its eggs in cotton bolls or buds, causing great damage.

brigade—military force made up of two or more large groups with its own headquarters.

Bryan, William Jennings—(1860–1925) Democratic leader, secretary of state, public speaker, and lawyer. He ran unsuccessfully three times for the U.S. presidency (1896, 1900, 1908) and was thought to be a politician concerned with the problems of the common people.

Butler Act—law adopted in Tennessee in March 1925 that made it illegal to teach the theory of evolution in public schools.

Civilian Conservation Corps—(CCC) New Deal program (1933–1942) that provided jobs for young men doing forestry and conservation work.

conveyor belt—moving surface that carries necessary material to workers who then do not have to move themselves.

convicted—found guilty by a court of law.

Coolidge, Calvin—(1872–1933) president of the United States from 1923 until early 1929. The country enjoyed good economic times during his presidency.

corset—stiff undergarment meant to give support or shape to a woman's body. It is very uncomfortable, tight, and confining.

The Crisis—official magazine of the National Association for the Advancement of Colored People (NAACP), edited by W.E.B. Du Bois. It was one of the most important publications of the Harlem Renaissance.

Darrow, Clarence—(1857–1938) famous American defense lawyer, public speaker, and writer who argued for the defense in the Scopes Trial.

Darwin, Charles—(1809–1882) British naturalist and author of *On the Origin of Species* (1859), which presented his theory of evolution.

dance marathon—type of contest. The winners were the couple who danced the longest without stopping.

The Defender—most influential African-American newspaper in the U.S. during the early 20th century. It played a leading role in the migration of African Americans from the South to the North.

defense—side in a trial that tries to prove that the accused person is not guilty.

depression—period during which businesses suffer and many people are out of work. (See also Great Depression.)

drought—long period of dry weather.

Dust Bowl—area of the American plains where poor farming methods and dry weather led to the wind carrying away millions of acres of soil in the 1930s.

Edgar Bergen-Charlie McCarthy program—popular radio program featuring ventriloquist Edgar Bergen (1903–1978) and his dummy Charlie McCarthy. It was America's most popular radio program in 1938.

empire—group of states or territories under one ruler.

epidemic—disease that spreads so rapidly that many people have it at one time.

erosion—wearing-away of land due to flooding, wind, or other natural causes.

ethnic group—people with a language, customs, and history in common.

evolution—theory that higher forms of life, including human beings, develop from simpler forms. The law against teaching this theory was passed by people who felt it goes against Bible teaching.

Fauset, Jessie Redmon—(1882–1961) novelist and literary editor of *The Crisis* from 1919 to 1926, during the time of the Harlem Renaissance.

Fitzgerald, F. Scott—(1896–1940) considered one of the top American writers of his time. His works, including *The Great Gatsby*, have forever captured the 1920s for readers.

flagpole sitters—people who sat on chairs at the tops of flagpoles, often for many days or weeks, to get attention and have fun.

flapper—young woman in the 1920s who broke the rules of behavior and dress.

Foch (FOSH), **Ferdinand**—(1851–1929) World War I commander of all British, French, and American forces in 1918.

folklore—traditional tales of a group of people, usually passed from person to person through storytelling instead of printed books.

Ford, Henry—(1863–1947) founder and owner of the Ford Motor Company. His use of the assembly line in his plants made Ford the world's largest automobile manufacturer in his day.

fundamentalist—person who believes that the Bible is a complete and accurate historical record and statement of prophecy; a strict observer of the basic principles of a religion.

Great Depression—worst economic period in American history. Lasting ten years, this depression caused as many as one out of every four workers to be without a job.

Great Migration—massive movement of African Americans from the South to the North in the early part of the 20th century. Most families came in search of work and freedom.

Great War—(1914–1918) term used to refer to World War I in the period before World War II.

Harlem—section of New York City in northern Manhattan.

Harlem Renaissance (HAR•lehm REHN•ih•sahns)—period of outstanding creativity that took place in Harlem, New York City, in the 1920s. Its main ideas included African-American racial pride, freedom, and equality.

Hoover, Herbert—(1874–1964) 31st president of the United States. Elected in 1928, Hoover was in office when America's economy went from the prosperity of the 1920s to the depression of the 1930s.

Hoovervilles—communities of sheds, tents, and cars where homeless people lived during the Depression. They were named after the president that many people blamed for their condition.

Hughes, Langston—(1902–1967) African-American poet and writer who was one of the star figures of the Harlem Renaissance.

Hurston, Zora Neale—(1903–1960) African-American folklorist and writer who celebrated the black culture of the Southern countryside.

inaugural address—speech given by a president at his inauguration, the ceremony in which he is sworn into office.

infantry—soldiers who fight on foot, usually with light weapons.

influenza—serious illness marked by fever, aches and pains, and coughing. It is spread by a virus that can be passed from person to person like a common cold.

jazz—type of popular American music; the forerunner of most American popular music today.

joint session—meeting at which members of both the House of Representatives and the Senate are present.

just war—war that is morally right. Most people agree that a war fought by a nation to defend itself or others is a just war.

Kaiser—ruler of the German empire. Wilhelm II (1859–1941) was emperor of Germany from 1888 to 1918.

Ku Klux Klan—group formed in 1886 that wanted to keep former slaves powerless.

Lange, Dorothea—(1895–1965) famous photographer of the American people during the 1930s.

latrines—toilets.

Lindbergh, Charles A.—(1902–1974) first person to fly nonstop alone across the Atlantic Ocean.

literary editor—person in charge of deciding which stories and poems a magazine publishes.

livelihood—way of making a living.

Lusitania—British passenger ship sunk by German submarines in May 1915. One hundred twenty-eight Americans were killed.

lynching—putting an accused person to death, usually by hanging, without a lawful trial.

martial (MAHR•shuhl) **law**—military rule of a country or other region in time of war or emergency.

McKay, Claude—(1890–1948) Jamaican-born poet and novelist whose *Home to Harlem* was the most popular book of fiction written by an African American of its time.

Medal of Honor—medal awarded by Congress for outstanding bravery in wartime.

migrant workers—people who move from place to place in order to find work.

New Deal—series of federal government programs designed to reverse the economic depression of the 1930s and to relieve poverty.

Nineteenth Amendment—amendment to the United States Constitution, passed in 1919, declaring that no one could be denied the right to vote based on sex.

over-grazed—referring to land that has had its plant life eaten away by livestock such as cattle and sheep.

"Over There"—patriotic World War I song. "There" was Europe, where Americans were shipped to fight the Germans.

periscope—instrument that uses mirrors to allow observation of objects that are not in a direct line of sight.

Phillips, Wendell—(1811–1884) crusader who spoke about the evils of slavery in the years leading up to the Civil War. A Chicago high school is named for him.

pneumonia (nuh•MOH•nyuh)—disease of the lungs that can result in death.

prosecution—side in a trial that tries to show that the accused person is guilty.

Rankin, Jeannette—(1880–1973) Montana native who, in 1916, was the first woman elected to the U. S. House of Representatives. Rankin voted "no" to the entry of the United States into World War I. In 1941 she cast the single "no" vote for declaring war against Japan.

refugees—people who flee a terrible situation such as war or drought in search of safety, or *refuge*.

relief—general name for the mixture of private, state, and federal programs that provide help to the poor.

River Rouge plant—Ford factory in Detroit, newly opened in 1927.

Roosevelt, Franklin—(1882–1945) 32nd president of the United States, elected first in 1932 and then three times after that. He helped the country get through both the Great Depression and World War II.

rouge (ROOZH)—makeup used to give a red color, usually to the cheeks and lips.

rural—country-like.

Ruth, Babe—(1895–1948) baseball player who was home run king of the 1920s. Some of his records were not broken until the 1960s and 1970s.

Scopes, John Thomas—(1900–1970) Dayton, Tennessee, high school teacher accused in 1925 of illegally teaching the theory of evolution to his students.

Secretary of the Interior—U.S. government official in charge of public lands who reports to the president.

Selective Service Act—law passed by Congress in May 1917 that required all men between the ages of 21 and 30 to sign up for military service.

sharecropper—person who farms land for the owner in return for part of the crops.

shell shock—condition suffered by many World War I soldiers who were not able to return to normal life. Shells were the kind of ammunition used by the large guns. Being close to their constant explosions was thought to have damaged the soldiers' minds.

Shenandoah National Park—forest of almost 200,000 acres located along the top of the Blue Ridge Mountains in northern Virginia.

sociologist—scientist who studies human social behavior.

sod—surface layer of soil covered with grasses.

speakeasy—place, like a club or bar, for the illegal sale of alcoholic drinks. Prohibition outlawed alcoholic beverages from 1920 to 1933.

spirituals—religious songs from African-American sources.

step-in—simple undergarment for women that is one piece from the shoulders to the legs.

stock market—place where stocks are bought and sold. Stocks allow people to own a piece of a company.

stockyard—place with pens and sheds to keep cattle, sheep, hogs, and horses before shipping or slaughtering them. Chicago had a great many stockyards in the early 1900s.

Studebaker—popular sports car for young people. It was often raced.

Stutz Bearcat—car popular in the 1920s.

suffrage—right to vote. The movement to get U.S. women the right to vote began with the Seneca Falls Convention (1848) for women's rights, organized by Elizabeth Cady Stanton and Lucretia Mott.

sustainable agriculture—farming that respects and protects the land so that future farmers can use it as well.

talkies—talking movies. In the late 1920s, silent movies were quickly replaced by ones with sound.

ticker tape—long ribbons of paper with stock market news and prices printed on them.

topsoil—surface soil of land, necessary for farming.

Trenton—capital of New Jersey, located in the west central part of the state, on its border with Pennsylvania.

urban—city-like.

vaccine—small amount of a disease that, when given to people (usually in a shot), prepares their body to fight the full disease if it needs to.

violating an unjust statute—breaking an unfair law.

virus—infectious disease caused by extremely small particles coated with protein. The particles are often not active until they come in contact with living cells.

"The War of the Worlds"—originally a science fiction book by English writer H. G. Wells in which Martians invade earth. Orson Welles's radio broadcast in 1938 caused major panic and demonstrated the power of radio.

Welles, Orson—(1915–1985) American filmmaker and actor. He became nationally famous as a result of "The War of the Worlds" broadcast. He next went to Hollywood, where he directed and starred in *Citizen Kane* (1941).

Wilhelm—(1859–1941) emperor of Germany from 1888 to 1918.

Wilson, Woodrow—(1856–1924) 28th president of the United States (1913–1921). He was awarded the Nobel Peace Prize for his efforts to end World War I and establish the League of Nations.

World War I—(1914–1918) war that involved more countries and caused greater destruction than any previous war. Nearly ten million troops died. The war cost the fighting nations more than $300 billion.

World War II—(1939–1945) war between the Axis powers (Germany, Italy, and Japan) and the Allies (England, the Soviet Union, France, China, and the United States). It broke out September 1, 1939, when Germany invaded Poland, and ended with the surrender of Germany and Japan in 1945.

York, Alvin—(1887–1964) American hero of World War I. As a corporal he captured 132 Germans almost singlehandedly.

Acknowledgements

10 Courtesy of the Library of Congress.
16 © Corbis.
17 © Tulane University.
20, 22, 23 Courtesy of the Library of Congress.
25 © Museum of Modern Art, New York.
29, 34, 38 Courtesy of the Library of Congress.
42 Courtesy of the National Archives, College Park.
52, 58, 65 Courtesy of the Library of Congress.
68 Courtesy of the National Archives, College Park.
78, 86, 91, 93, 101, 105, 116 Courtesy of the Library of Congress.
119, 125 © The Schomburg Center for Reseach in Black Culture.

127, 132, 142, 148, 154, 157, 164, 168, 174, 179, 183, 187 Courtesy of the Library of Congress.
189, 192 © The Dorothea Lange Collection, Oakland Museum of California, City of Oakland, Gift of Paul S. Taylor.
193 © Corbis.
195 © The Dorothea Lange Collection, Oakland Museum of California, City of Oakland, Gift of Paul S. Taylor.
196 © The New York Public Library.
198 © The Dorothea Lange Collection, Oakland Museum of California, City of Oakland, Gift of Paul S. Taylor.
201 Courtesy of the National Archives, College Park.
208, 209 Courtesy of the Library of Congress.